# Unit Resource Guide
# Unit 9
## Connections to Division

THIRD EDITION

KENDALL/HUNT PUBLISHING COMPANY
4050 Westmark Drive Dubuque, Iowa 52002

A TIMS® Curriculum
University of Illinois at Chicago

**UIC** The University of Illinois at Chicago

The original edition was based on work supported by the National Science Foundation under grant No. MDR 9050226 and the University of Illinois at Chicago. Any opinions, findings, and conclusions or recommendations expressed in this publication are those of the author(s) and do not necessarily reflect the views of the granting agencies.



ISBN 978-0-7575-3624-3



Printed in the United States of America

1 2 3 4 5 6 7 8 9 10 11 10 09 08 07

# Letter Home

## Connections to Division

Date: ____________________

Dear Family Member:

In this unit, students review paper-and-pencil methods for dividing, and division is extended to two-digit divisors. Students will solve many division word problems and interpret the remainders. They will also learn strategies for solving real-world problems using a calculator and make further connections between division and fractions. Students will complete an assessment activity using estimation and multiplication to find the number of blades of grass in a given area.

```
      22 R3
24 | 531    |
   - 480    | 20
      51    |
   -  48    |  2
       3      22
```

A method for division with a two-digit divisor

You can help at home by encouraging your child to explain to you how he or she is learning to divide.

Sincerely,

______________________________________________

# Carta al hogar

## Conexiones con la división

Fecha: ____________________

Estimado miembro de familia:

En esta unidad, los estudiantes repasarán métodos de papel y lápiz para dividir. La división se extenderá a divisores de dos dígitos. Los estudiantes resolverán problemas razonados e interpretarán los residuos. También aprenderán estrategias para resolver problemas del mundo real usando una calculadora, y establecerán más conexiones entre la división y las fracciones. Los estudiantes también completarán una actividad de evaluación en la que usarán la estimación y la multiplicación para hallar el número de hojas de zacate en un área determinada.

```
      22 R3
24 | 531
   - 480   | 20
      51   |
   -  48   |  2
       3     22
```

Un método para dividir con un divisor de dos dígitos

Usted puede ayudar a su hijo/a en casa animándole a que le explique cómo está aprendiendo a dividir.

Atentamente,

______________________________________________

# Table of Contents

## Unit 9
## Connections to Division

# Outline

## Connections to Division

### Unit Summary

*Estimated Class Sessions*
**10-12**

This unit focuses on division and its applications. Students explore the relationship between fractions and division to find decimal equivalents for fractions. They extend paper-and-pencil division to two-digit divisors and interpret remainders.

An optional activity introduces a different multiplication method: lattice multiplication. The lattice method is connected to the compact and all-partials algorithms. Students use calculators to divide larger numbers and devise strategies to find whole number remainders with calculators.

To conclude the unit, students solve an open-response problem in which they estimate the number of blades of grass in a lawn. They use the Student Rubrics to help them communicate their solution strategies.

### Major Concept Focus

- fractions and division
- decimal equivalents for fractions
- paper-and-pencil division
- interpreting remainders
- checking division with multiplication
- estimating quotients
- using multiplication and division to solve problems
- calculator strategies for dividing
- repeating decimals
- communicating solution strategies
- measuring area
- Student Rubric: *Knowing*
- Student Rubric: *Solving*
- Student Rubric: *Telling*

## Pacing Suggestions

- Use the recommended number of sessions for each lesson as a guide. Students extend their division skills in this unit, but it is not necessary to wait until all students master each concept and skill. Distributed practice of small sets of division problems and sets of word problems are included in each succeeding unit in the Daily Practice and Problems and Home Practice.
- Lesson 3 *Multiplication Methods* is an optional lesson that challenges students to learn different methods for multiplication. You can use this lesson as an extension.

## Assessment Indicators

Use the following Assessment Indicators and the *Observational Assessment Record* that follows the Background section in this unit to assess students on key ideas.

**A1.** Can students divide with 2-digit divisors using paper and pencil?

**A2.** Can students estimate quotients?

**A3.** Can students interpret remainders?

**A4.** Can students write quotients as mixed numbers?

**A5.** Can students use a calculator to solve division problems?

**A6.** Can students check division using multiplication?

**A7.** Can students solve open-response problems and communicate solution strategies?

**A8.** Can students find decimal equivalents for fractions?

# Unit Planner

**KEY:** SG = Student Guide, DAB = Discovery Assignment Book, AB = Adventure Book, URG = Unit Resource Guide, DPP = Daily Practice and Problems, HP = Home Practice (found in Discovery Assignment Book), and TIG = Teacher Implementation Guide.

| | Lesson Information | Supplies | Copies/ Transparencies |
|---|---|---|---|
| **Lesson 1**<br>**Fractions and Division**<br>URG Pages 27–46<br>SG Pages 286–293<br>DAB Pages 151–152<br>DPP A–D<br>HP Part 1<br>*Estimated Class Sessions* **2** | **Activity**<br>Students explore the relationship between division sentences and fractions. Students use calculators to change fractions into their decimal equivalents or approximations and compare them. Repeating decimals are introduced.<br>**Homework**<br>1. Assign the *Dividing Pizzas* Homework Pages in the *Discovery Assignment Book* after Part 1 of the lesson.<br>2. Assign the Homework section in the *Student Guide*.<br>3. Assign Part 1 of the Home Practice.<br>**Assessment**<br>1. Use some of the questions on the homework pages as assessments. ***Question 3*** on the *Dividing Pizzas* Homework Pages and ***Questions 2–4*** in the *Student Guide* Homework section are good choices.<br>2. Use the *Observational Assessment Record* to note students' abilities to find decimal equivalents for fractions. | • 1 small centiwheel per student<br>• 1 calculator per student | • 1 wheel from *Small Centiwheels* URG Page 38 per student, optional<br>• 1 copy of *Centimeter Dot Paper* URG Page 39 per student, optional<br>• 1 copy of *Observational Assessment Record* URG Pages 11–12 to be used throughout this unit |
| **Lesson 2**<br>**Division**<br>URG Pages 47–63<br>SG Pages 294–298<br>DAB Pages 153–155<br>DPP E–J<br>HP Part 2<br>*Estimated Class Sessions* **3** | **Activity**<br>Students review a method for dividing. Estimation strategies are emphasized. Students use multiplication to check their work.<br>**Math Facts**<br>DPP item G provides practice with the division facts for the 5s and 10s.<br>**Homework**<br>1. Assign the *More Estimation and Division* Activity Page in the *Discovery Assignment Book*.<br>2. Assign the Homework section in the *Student Guide*.<br>3. Assign Part 2 of the Home Practice.<br>4. Assign DPP Task J.<br>**Assessment**<br>1. Use the Homework section of the *Student Guide* as an assessment.<br>2. Use the *Observational Assessment Record* to note students' abilities to estimate quotients and to divide using a paper-and-pencil method. | • base-ten pieces, optional | • 1 transparency of *Introducing Division* URG Page 58, optional |

| | Lesson Information | Supplies | Copies/ Transparencies |
|---|---|---|---|
| **Lesson 3**<br>**Multiplication Methods**<br>URG Pages 64–73<br>SG Pages 299–303<br>DAB Pages 157–158<br>*Estimated Class Sessions* **2** | OPTIONAL LESSON—EXTENSION<br>**Optional Activity**<br>Students use paper-and-pencil methods for multiplying larger numbers. A new method, lattice multiplication, is introduced. Students compare multiplication methods.<br>**Homework**<br>1. Assign the *Lattice Multiplication Practice* Activity Pages.<br>2. Assign the Homework section in the *Student Guide.* | | |
| **Lesson 4**<br>**Understanding Remainders**<br>URG Pages 74–87<br>SG Pages 304–309<br>DPP K–N<br>HP Parts 3–4<br>*Estimated Class Sessions* **2** | **Activity**<br>Students explore remainders in division problems. Students complete division problems in which the remainder is expressed as a fraction.<br>**Math Facts**<br>DPP items K and M review the multiplication and division facts for the 5s and 10s.<br>**Homework**<br>1. Assign ***Questions 4–9*** on the *Understanding Remainders* Activity Pages.<br>2. Assign homework ***Questions 1–10*** in the *Student Guide.*<br>3. Assign Parts 3 and 4 of the Home Practice.<br>**Assessment**<br>1. Students complete the *Tie Dye T-Shirts* Assessment Page.<br>2. Use DPP Task N as a quiz<br>3. Use the *Observational Assessment Record* to note students' abilities to interpret remainders. | | • 1 copy of *Tie Dye T-Shirts* URG Page 82 per student |
| **Lesson 5**<br>**Calculator Strategies: Division**<br>URG Pages 88–97<br>SG Pages 310–313<br>DPP O–P<br>HP Part 5<br>*Estimated Class Sessions* **1** | **Activity**<br>Students use calculators to divide larger numbers. They divide money using a calculator so the quotient reflects both dollars and cents.<br>**Homework**<br>1. Assign homework ***Questions 1–10*** in the *Student Guide.*<br>2. Assign Part 5 of the Home Practice.<br>**Assessment**<br>1. Use homework ***Questions 1*** and ***9*** in the *Student Guide* as an assessment.<br>2. Use the *Observational Assessment Record* to note students' abilities to use a calculator to solve division problems. | • 1 calculator per student | |

*(Continued)*

| | Lesson Information | Supplies | Copies/ Transparencies |
|---|---|---|---|
| **Lesson 6**<br>**Grass Act**<br>URG Pages 98–114<br>SG Page 314<br>DPP Q–T<br>*Estimated Class Sessions* **2** | **Assessment Activity**<br>Students solve an open-response problem and write their solution strategies. They estimate the number of blades of grass in a given area.<br>**Math Facts**<br>DPP items Q and S practice the facts for the 5s and 10s.<br>**Homework**<br>Assign the Journal Prompt for homework.<br>**Assessment**<br>1. Use DPP Challenge T as an assessment of concepts learned in this unit.<br>2. Transfer appropriate documentation from the Unit 9 *Observational Assessment Record* to students' *Individual Assessment Record Sheets.* | • 1 pair of scissors per student group<br>• 1 3" by 5" index card per student<br>• 1 ruler per student group<br>• 1 calculator per student<br>• a large grassy area or piece of sod, nylon netting, window screen, or large beach towel | • 1 copy of *Grass Act Questions* URG Page 113 per student<br>• 1 copy of *TIMS Multidimensional Rubric* TIG, Assessment section<br>• 1 transparency or poster of Student Rubrics: *Solving, Knowing,* and *Telling* TIG, Assessment section, optional<br>• 1 copy of *Individual Assessment Record Sheet* TIG Assessment section per student, previously copied for use throughout the year |

## Connections

A current list of literature and software connections is available at *www.mathtrailblazers.com.* You can also find information on connections in the *Teacher Implementation Guide* Literature List and Software List sections.

### Literature Connections

#### Suggested Titles

- Wilder, Laura Ingalls. *Little House in the Big Woods.* HarperCollins, New York, 2001. (Lesson 1)

### Software Connections

- *Fraction Attraction* develops understanding of fractions using fraction bars, pie charts, hundreds blocks, and other materials.
- *Math Munchers Deluxe* provides practice in basic facts and finding equivalent fractions, decimals, percents, ratios, angles and identifying geometric shapes, factors and multiples in an arcade-like game.
- *Mighty Math Calculating Crew* poses short answer questions about number operations, 3-dimensional shapes, and money skills.
- *Mighty Math Number Heroes* poses short answer questions about fractions, number operations, polygons, and probability.
- *Number Sense and Problem Solving: How the West Was One + Three × Four* provides practice with the order of operations.
- *Tenth Planet: Fraction Operations* develops conceptual understanding of fraction operations, including finding common denominators.

# Teaching All Math Trailblazers Students

*Math Trailblazers*® lessons are designed for students with a wide range of abilities. The lessons are flexible and do not require significant adaptation for diverse learning styles or academic levels. However, when needed, lessons can be tailored to allow students to engage their abilities to the greatest extent possible while building knowledge and skills.

To assist you in meeting the needs of all students in your classroom, this section contains information about some of the features in the curriculum that allow all students access to mathematics. For additional information, see the Teaching the *Math Trailblazers* Student: Meeting Individual Needs section in the *Teacher Implementation Guide.*

## Differentiation Opportunities in this Unit

### Games

Use games to promote or extend understanding of math concepts and to practice skills with children who need more practice.

- *Digits Game: Addition with Decimals* from DPP Task L in Lesson 4 *Understanding Remainders*
- *Digits Game: Subtraction with Decimals* from DPP Task P in Lesson 5 *Calculator Strategies: Division*

### Journal Prompts

Journal prompts provide opportunities for students to explain and reflect on mathematical problems. They can help both students who need practice explaining their ideas and students who benefit from answering higher order questions. Students with various learning styles can express themselves using pictures, words, and sentences. Teachers can alter journal prompts to suit students' ability levels. The following lessons contain a journal prompt:

- Lesson 1 *Fractions and Division*
- Lesson 2 *Division*
- Lesson 3 *Multiplication Methods*
- Lesson 4 *Understanding Remainders*
- Lesson 6 *Grass Act*

### DPP Challenges

DPP Challenges are items from the Daily Practice and Problems that usually take more than fifteen minutes to complete. These problems are more thought-provoking and can be used to stretch students' problem-solving skills. The following lessons have DPP Challenges in them:

- DPP Challenge D from Lesson 1 *Fractions and Division*
- DPP Challenges F and H from Lesson 2 *Division*
- DPP Challenge T from Lesson 6 *Grass Act*

### Extensions

Use extensions to enrich lessons. Many extensions provide opportunities to further involve or challenge students of all abilities. Take a moment to review the extensions prior to beginning this unit. Some extensions may require additional preparation and planning. The following lesson contains an extension:

- Lesson 5 *Calculator Strategies: Division*

# Background

## Connections to Division

"Instructional programs from prekindergarten to grade 12 should enable all students to compute fluently and make reasonable estimates.

"Developing fluency requires a balance and connection between conceptual understanding and computational proficiency. On the one hand, computational methods that are over-practiced without understanding are often forgotten or remembered incorrectly (Hiebert 1999; Kamii, Lewis, and Livingston, 1993; Hiebert and Lindquist 1990). On the other hand, understanding without fluency can inhibit the problem-solving process (Thornton 1990).

"Part of being able to compute fluently means making smart choices about which tools to use and when. Students should have experiences that help them learn to choose among mental computation, paper-and-pencil strategies, estimation, and calculator use. The particular context, the question, and the numbers involved all play roles in those choices. Do the numbers allow a mental strategy? Does the context call for an estimate? Does the problem require repeated and tedious computations? Students should evaluate problem situations to determine whether an estimate or an exact answer is needed, using their number sense to advantage, and be able to give a rationale for their decision."

From the National Council of Teachers of Mathematics *Principles and Standards for School Mathematics,* 2000.

The activities in this unit reinforce students' conceptual understanding of division. Children further investigate how fractions and division connect and how to interpret division done on a calculator. Fluency with division using a paper-and-pencil method does not ensure that students will know when to use division. Therefore, we provide a variety of problem contexts in which division is the most efficient operation for finding a solution to the problem.

Since problems are presented in contexts, students must use the information given to decide how to interpret the remainder. They also learn to express a quotient as a mixed number. The forgiving method—the paper-and-pencil division method discussed in Unit 4—is reviewed and extended to include two-digit divisors. Students are encouraged to continue to use mental math to divide round numbers and to use efficient estimation strategies as they divide larger numbers.

As students solve problems involving larger numbers, they need to develop facility with calculators. Using calculators requires students to understand the arithmetic processes called for in each situation. They must also use estimation to determine if the solution on the calculator display is reasonable. Using calculators also provides students with the resources needed to solve more interesting and complex problems efficiently.

This unit provides many practice problems for multiplying and dividing. These should be assigned conservatively. It is better for children to do a few problems at a time so they have time to think and internalize the concepts behind the computations.

Students review paper-and-pencil multiplication in the context of checking division. In an optional activity, students can extend their knowledge of multiplication by learning a classic method called lattice multiplication. This method has been known and used for more than 500 years. Students also use multiplication in an open-response assessment problem that requires problem-solving, estimation, and communication skills.

## Resources


- Burns, Marilyn. *About Teaching Mathematics. A K–8 Resource.* Math Solutions Publications, White Plains, NY, 1992.
- Hiebert, James. "Relationships between Research and the NCTM Standards." *Journal for Research in Mathematics Education* 30, pp. 3–19, January 1999.
- Hiebert, James, and Mary Lindquist. "Developing Mathematical Knowledge in the Young Child" in *Mathematics for the Young Child,* edited by Joseph N. Payne, pp. 17–36. National Council of Teachers of Mathematics, Reston, VA, 1990.
- Kamii, Constance, Barbara A. Lewis, and Sally Jones Livingston. "Primary Arithmetic: Children Inventing Their Own Procedures." *Arithmetic Teacher* 41, pp. 200–203, December 1993.
- *Principles and Standards for School Mathematics,* National Council of Teachers of Mathematics, Reston, VA, 2000.
- Thornton, Carol A. "Strategies for the Basic Facts" in *Mathematics for the Young Child,* edited by Joseph N. Payne, pp. 133–51. National Council of Teachers of Mathematics, Reston, VA, 1990.

# Observational Assessment Record

- **A1** Can students divide with 2-digit divisors using paper and pencil?
- **A2** Can students estimate quotients?
- **A3** Can students interpret remainders?
- **A4** Can students write quotients as mixed numbers?
- **A5** Can students use a calculator to solve division problems?
- **A6** Can students check division using multiplication?
- **A7** Can students solve open-response problems and communicate solution strategies?
- **A8** Can students find decimal equivalents for fractions?
- **A9** ______________________________

| Name | A1 | A2 | A3 | A4 | A5 | A6 | A7 | A8 | A9 | Comments |
|---|---|---|---|---|---|---|---|---|---|---|
| 1. | | | | | | | | | | |
| 2. | | | | | | | | | | |
| 3. | | | | | | | | | | |
| 4. | | | | | | | | | | |
| 5. | | | | | | | | | | |
| 6. | | | | | | | | | | |
| 7. | | | | | | | | | | |
| 8. | | | | | | | | | | |
| 9. | | | | | | | | | | |
| 10. | | | | | | | | | | |
| 11. | | | | | | | | | | |
| 12. | | | | | | | | | | |
| 13. | | | | | | | | | | |

| Name | A1 | A2 | A3 | A4 | A5 | A6 | A7 | A8 | A9 | Comments |
|---|---|---|---|---|---|---|---|---|---|---|
| 14. | | | | | | | | | | |
| 15. | | | | | | | | | | |
| 16. | | | | | | | | | | |
| 17. | | | | | | | | | | |
| 18. | | | | | | | | | | |
| 19. | | | | | | | | | | |
| 20. | | | | | | | | | | |
| 21. | | | | | | | | | | |
| 22. | | | | | | | | | | |
| 23. | | | | | | | | | | |
| 24. | | | | | | | | | | |
| 25. | | | | | | | | | | |
| 26. | | | | | | | | | | |
| 27. | | | | | | | | | | |
| 28. | | | | | | | | | | |
| 29. | | | | | | | | | | |
| 30. | | | | | | | | | | |
| 31. | | | | | | | | | | |
| 32. | | | | | | | | | | |

# Daily Practice and Problems

## Connections to Division

## A DPP Menu for Unit 9

Two Daily Practice and Problems (DPP) items are included for each class session listed in the Unit Outline. A scope and sequence chart for the DPP is in the *Teacher Implementation Guide.*

Icons in the Teacher Notes column designate the subject matter of each DPP item. The first item in each class session is always a Bit and the second is either a Task or Challenge. Each item falls into one or more of the categories listed below. A menu of the DPP items for Unit 9 follows.

| Number Sense | Computation | Time | Geometry |
|---|---|---|---|
| C, E–G, I, L–R, T | A, C, H, J, L–R, T | B | |
| **Math Facts** | **Money** | **Measurement** | **Data** |
| G, K, M, Q, S | C, H | H | D |

The *Daily Practice and Problems and Home Practice Guide* in the *Teacher Implementation Guide* includes information on how and when to use the DPP.

### Review of Math Facts

In the first half of the year, DPP items reviewed the multiplication and division facts through work with fact families (e.g., $3 \times 5 = 15$ and $5 \times 3 = 15$, so $15 \div 3 = 5$ and $15 \div 5 = 3$). Students will continue to review the facts as part of the Daily Practice and Problems.

The table lists the groups of facts and when each is studied throughout the DPP in Units 9–16.

The DPP for this unit reviews the facts for the 5s and 10s. See Items G, K, M, Q, and S.

For a detailed explanation of our approach to learning the facts, see the *Grade 5 Facts Resource Guide* and the TIMS Tutor: *Math Facts* in the *Teacher Implementation Guide.* Also, see the *Math Facts Philosophy: Information for Parents,* which immediately follows the Unit 2 Background.

| Unit | Distribution of Multiplication and Division Facts |
|---|---|
| 9 | 5s and 10s |
| 10 | 2s and squares |
| 11 | 3s and 9s |
| 12 | Last six facts |
| 13 | 2s, 5s, 10s, and squares |
| 14 | 3s, 9s, and last six facts |
| 15 | Review all facts. |
| 16 | Review all facts. |

# Daily Practice and Problems

**Students may solve the items individually, in groups, or as a class. The items may also be assigned for homework. The DPPs are also available on the Teacher Resource CD.**

## Student Questions

### A Division Practice

Use paper and pencil or mental math to solve the following problems. Estimate to be sure your answer is reasonable.

A. $678 \div 4 =$

B. $200 \div 5 =$

C. $56 \div 5 =$

D. $1264 \div 8 =$

## Teacher Notes

### TIMS Bit

A. 169 R2

B. 40

C. 11 R1

D. 158

## Student Questions

### B Arrival Time

Los Angeles is in the Pacific Standard Time (PST) zone and New York is in the Eastern Standard Time (EST) zone. When it is noon in Los Angeles, it is 3:00 P.M. in New York.

A plane leaves New York at 8:30 A.M. and takes 5 hours to fly to Los Angeles. The time in Los Angeles is always 3 hours earlier than New York. What time will the plane arrive in Los Angeles?

## Teacher Notes

### TIMS Task

**10:30 A.M.**

**Time change is a difficult concept for some students. Looking at a time zone map of the United States will help. Daylight savings time further complicates the idea because not all areas of the United States change their clocks. Ignore this fact for this problem.**

**Student Questions** | **Teacher Notes**

## Bargain Shopping

Frank needs to buy school supplies. He needs four of each item. For each item, help Frank decide whether he will save money by buying the items in packs or individually. Figure out how much he will save on each item. Then, find his total savings.

| Item | Packs of 4 | Individual |
|---|---|---|
| pencils | 18¢ | 4¢ |
| rulers | 98¢ | 25¢ |
| folders | 45¢ | 12¢ |
| crayons | 29¢ | 7¢ |
| pens | $1.40 | 36¢ |

### TIMS Bit

pencils—individual; savings of 2¢

rulers—pack; savings of 2¢

folders—pack; savings of 3¢

crayons—individual; savings of 1¢

pens—pack; savings of 4¢

Total savings of 12¢.

## Arranging Colors

Lee Yah received three different-colored sweatshirts for her birthday—blue, red, and yellow. She is deciding which one to wear to school on Monday, Tuesday, and Wednesday.

1. In what order can she wear the three sweatshirts? List all the different ways.
2. If Lee Yah decides to wear the blue sweatshirt on Monday, in what order can she wear the other two shirts? List all possibilities.
3. If she chooses not to wear the blue and yellow sweatshirts in a row (not blue, yellow and not yellow, blue), in what order could she wear the three sweat-shirts? List all the different ways.

### TIMS Challenge

1. 6 ways: RYB, RBY, BYR, BRY, YRB, YBR
2. 2 ways: YR or RY
3. 2 ways: BRY or YRB

| Student Questions | Teacher Notes |
|---|---|

## Estimating with Ease

See if you can figure out these problems in your head. Then write down your reasoning for each answer.

1. About how many 12s are in 140?

2. About how many 25s are in 370?

3. About how many 20s are in 345?

### TIMS Bit

**Answers will vary but should include students' thinking strategies. Sharing these strategies with the class, or in groups, will allow students to see several ways of figuring estimates.**

1. **10 or 11 are good estimates.**
2. **14 or 15 are good estimates. $25 \times 10 = 250$ Then, skip count by 25s—275, 300, 325, 350—for a total of fourteen 25s. Alternatively, there are four 25s in 100 so there are twelve 25s in 300. Add on three more 25s for a total of 15 $(300 + 25 + 25 + 25 = 375)$.**
3. **15, 16, or 17 are good estimates. There are five 20s in 100 so there are fifteen 20s in 300. It takes 2 more 20s to reach 340 for a total of 17. Alternatively, $20 \times 10 = 200$ and $20 \times 20 = 400$. Since 345 is about halfway between 200 and 400, 15 is a good estimate.**

| Student Questions | Teacher Notes |
|---|---|

## F Tenths, Hundredths, and Thousandths

1. Name a decimal that is greater than 0.3 but less than 0.35.
2. Name a decimal that is greater than 0.25 but less than 0.26.
3. Name a decimal that is greater than 0.403 but less than 0.41.
4. Name a fraction that is greater than $\frac{57}{100}$ but less than $\frac{7}{10}$.
5. Name a fraction that is greater than $\frac{8}{16}$ but less than 0.8.
6. Name a fraction that is greater than 17% but less than 0.2.

### TIMS Challenge 

**One example is provided for each. Encourage students to use grids from Unit 7 or picture them in their minds.**

1. 0.33
2. 0.254
3. .409
4. $\frac{6}{10}$ or $\frac{60}{100}$
5. $\frac{7}{10}$
6. $\frac{18}{100}$

## G Practicing the Facts

A. $300 \div 50 =$

B. $400 \div 4 =$

C. $150 \div 3 =$

D. $100 \div 10 =$

E. $45 \div 5 =$

F. $2500 \div 5 =$

G. $600 \div 100 =$

H. $35 \div 7 =$

I. $10 \div 5 =$

### TIMS Bit  

A. 6

B. 100

C. 50

D. 10

E. 9

F. 500

G. 6

H. 5

I. 2

| Student Questions | Teacher Notes |
|---|---|

## Craft Fair

1. Lee Yah and Manny are setting up tables for the fifth-grade family craft show. Each table is 200 cm long. Tables will line up along two sides of the room. Both sides of the room are 12 meters long. Each participant who wishes to sell crafts pays a $15 rental fee for one table or $25 for two tables. Mr. Moreno tells the students that all the tables are rented. Only 2 people rented two tables. How much money will the school make on the craft show?

2. The community craft show will be held in the gym next month. The school is charging $25 for one table and will have five times as many tables as the fifth-grade craft show. How much will the school make for hosting the community craft show if all of the tables are rented?

### TIMS Challenge

1. **$170; There are 12 tables. 8 people pay $15. 2 people pay $25.**
2. **$1500**

## Fractions, Decimals, and the Calculator

Use a calculator to change each of the following fractions to decimals. Then compare the decimals to see if each pair of fractions are equivalent.

A. $\frac{4}{7}$ and $\frac{3}{5}$

B. $\frac{1}{3}$ and $\frac{13}{39}$

C. $\frac{12}{15}$ and $\frac{8}{11}$

### TIMS Bit

A. $\frac{4}{7} \neq \frac{3}{5}$ since $\frac{4}{7} \approx .57$ and $\frac{3}{5} = .6$

B. $\frac{1}{3} = \frac{13}{39}$

C. $\frac{12}{15} \neq \frac{8}{11}$ since $\frac{12}{15} = .8$ and $\frac{8}{11} \approx .73$

| Student Questions | Teacher Notes |
|---|---|

## Division Practice

Use estimation to help you divide. Use a paper-and-pencil method or mental math. Show how you check your work.

A. $23\overline{)756}$ B. $20\overline{)4000}$

C. $42\overline{)8973}$ D. $75\overline{)684}$

### TIMS Task

A. 32 R20
$32 \times 23 + 20 = 756$

B. 200
$20 \times 200 = 4000$

C. 213 R27
$213 \times 42 + 27 = 8973$

D. 9 R9
$9 \times 75 + 9 = 684$

## More Fact Practice

Find $n$ to make each number sentence true.

A. $n \times 5 = 40$ B. $n \times 7 = 70$

C. $n \div 4 = 5$ D. $80 \div n = 10$

E. $10 \times n = 50$ F. $30 \div 5 = n$

G. $9 \times 10 = n$ H. $15 \div n = 5$

I. $n \times 8 = 80$

### TIMS Bit

A. 8 B. 10

C. 20 D. 8

E. 5 F. 6

G. 90 H. 3

I. 10

| Student Questions | Teacher Notes |
|---|---|

### *Digits Game:* Addition with Decimals

Draw boxes like these on your paper.

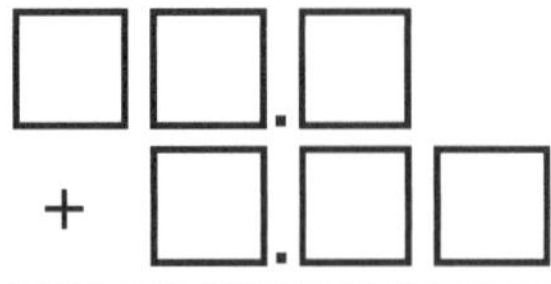

As your teacher or classmate chooses digits from a deck of digit cards, place them in the boxes. Try to make the largest sum. Remember, each digit will be read only once. Once you place a digit, it cannot be moved.

### TIMS Task

To begin the game, students draw the set of boxes on their papers. You choose a digit at random from a set of *Digit Cards (0–9)*. (*Digit Cards* follow item T in the *Unit Resource Guide.* As an alternative, use a deck of playing cards. The ace can stand for 1 and the joker or a face card can stand for zero.) Students place the digit in a box to try to get the largest sum. Once a digit is placed, it cannot be moved. Then you choose a second digit without replacing the first in the deck. Play continues until there are enough digits to fill the boxes. The player with the largest sum wins. Play again; however, this time students try to make the smallest sum.

### Multiplying and Dividing by Multiples of Ten

A. $80 \times 500 =$

B. $60 \times 100 =$

C. $20 \times 5000 =$

D. $3000 \div 60 =$

E. $70{,}000 \div 100 =$

F. $4500 \div 90 =$

### TIMS Bit

A. 40,000

B. 6000

C. 100,000

D. 50

E. 700

F. 50

| Student Questions | Teacher Notes |
|---|---|

## Operations

Use paper and pencil or mental math, not your calculator, to solve these problems. Write any remainders as whole numbers. When you finish a problem, look back to see if your answer is reasonable.

A. $59 \times 14 =$

B. $86 \times 42 =$

C. $409 \times 4 =$

D. $2486 \div 4 =$

E. $2486 \div 14 =$

F. $1067 \div 37 =$

### TIMS Task

A. 826

B. 3612

C. 1636

D. 621 R2

E. 177 R8

F. 28 R31

## Estimate the Products

Estimate the products. Be prepared to share how you estimated.

A. $4.2 \times 53 =$

B. $0.63 \times 0.18 =$

C. $0.25 \times 119 =$

D. $19 \times 81.56 =$

E. $2.09 \times 3.982 =$

F. $66 \times 9.09 =$

### TIMS Bit

Accept all reasonable answers. It's important for students to hear how other students estimate. One possible estimate is listed for each.

A. $4 \times 50 = 200$

B. $\frac{1}{2}$ of 0.18 is 0.09

C. $\frac{1}{4}$ of 120 is 30

D. $20 \times 80 = 1600$

E. $2 \times 4 = 8$

F. $66 \times 10 = 660$

| Student Questions | Teacher Notes |
|---|---|

### *Digits Game:* Subtraction with Decimals

Draw boxes like these on your paper.

$$\begin{array}{r} \square\square.\square \\ -\ \square.\square\square \\ \hline \end{array}$$

As your teacher or classmate chooses digits from a deck of digit cards, place them in the boxes. Try to make the largest difference. Remember, each digit will be read only once. Once you place a digit, it cannot be moved.

### TIMS Task

To begin the game, students draw the set of boxes on their papers. You choose a digit at random from a set of *Digit Cards (0–9)*. (*Digit Cards* follow DPP item T in the *Unit Resource Guide*. As an alternative, use a deck of playing cards. The ace can stand for 1 and the joker or a face card can stand for zero.) Students place the digit in a box to try to get the largest difference. Once a digit is placed, it cannot be moved. Then you choose a second digit without replacing the first in the deck. Play continues until there are enough digits to fill the boxes. The player with the largest difference wins. Play again; however, this time students try to make the smallest difference.

### Q Dividing by Multiples of Ten

A. 9000 ÷ 100 =

B. 45,000 ÷ 900 =

C. 20,000 ÷ 2 =

D. 350 ÷ 70 =

E. 250,000 ÷ 500 =

F. 30,000 ÷ 30 =

### TIMS Bit

A. 90

B. 50

C. 10,000

D. 5

E. 500

F. 1000

| Student Questions | Teacher Notes |
|---|---|

## Thinking about Remainders

1. You are dividing a number by 6 and at the end of the problem your remainder is 7. What does that mean?

2. Make a list of the possible remainders you can have when you finish dividing a number by 8.

### TIMS Task

1. It means that 6 can be divided into the dividend 1 more time. You are not finished dividing.
2. 0–7

## S Reviewing Division Facts: 5s and 10s

A. 45 ÷ 5 =

B. 25 ÷ 5 =

C. 10 ÷ 2 =

D. 60 ÷ 10 =

E. 40 ÷ 8 =

F. 30 ÷ 3 =

G. 20 ÷ 5 =

H. 80 ÷ 10 =

I. 30 ÷ 6 =

J. 35 ÷ 5 =

K. 15 ÷ 3 =

L. 50 ÷ 10 =

M. 70 ÷ 10 =

N. 90 ÷ 9 =

O. 40 ÷ 4 =

P. 20 ÷ 2 =

Q. 100 ÷ 10 =

### TIMS Bit

A. 9 B. 5
C. 5 D. 6
E. 5 F. 10
G. 4 H. 8
I. 5 J. 7
K. 5 L. 5
M. 7 N. 10
O. 10 P. 10
Q. 10

| Student Questions | Teacher Notes |
|---|---|

## Remainders

1. Solve each of the following problems. Each one has a remainder. Write the quotient three ways: with a whole number remainder, as a mixed number, and as a decimal.

   A. $6 \div 4 =$  B. $19 \div 4 =$

   C. $49 \div 4 =$

2. Choose one of the problems. Write 3 different stories for the problem showing how you might use each of the three types of quotients.

## TIMS Challenge  

**Students will need calculators to complete this challenge.**

1. **A.** 1 R2; $1\frac{1}{2}$; 1.5

   **B.** 4 R3; $4\frac{3}{4}$; 4.75

   **C.** 12 R1; $12\frac{1}{4}$; 12.25

2. One possible answer is given.

   $6 \div 4 = 1$ R2; to share 6 pencils among 4 students you would need to give each student 1 pencil. Two pencils would be left over.

   $6 \div 4 = 1\frac{1}{2}$; to share 6 cookies among 4 students you could give each student $1\frac{1}{2}$ cookies.

   $6 \div 4 = 1.5$; to share $6 among 4 students, you would need to give each student $1.50.

Name ______________________ Date ______________

# Digit Cards 0–9

| | |
|---|---|
| 4 | 9 |
| 3 | 8 |
| 2 | 7 |
| 1 | 6 |
| 0 | 5 |

Name ______________________ Date ______________

# Reverse Side of Digit Cards 0–9

# Fractions and Division

## Lesson Overview

*Estimated Class Sessions*

**2**

Students use pictures to explore the relationship between fractions and division. They use the small centiwheel and a calculator to find decimal equivalents (or decimal approximations) for fractions.

### Key Content

- Interpreting fractions as division.
- Finding decimal equivalents (or decimal approximations) for fractions using the small centiwheel.
- Finding decimal equivalents (or decimal approximations) for fractions using calculators.
- Identifying repeating decimals.

### Key Vocabulary

- repeating decimals

### Homework

1. Assign the *Dividing Pizzas* Homework Pages in the *Discovery Assignment Book* after Part 1 of the lesson.
2. Assign the Homework section in the *Student Guide.*
3. Assign Part 1 of the Home Practice.

### Assessment

1. Use some of the questions on the homework pages as assessments. ***Question 3*** on the *Dividing Pizzas* Homework Pages and ***Questions 2–4*** in the *Student Guide* Homework section are good choices.
2. Use the *Observational Assessment Record* to note students' abilities to find decimal equivalents for fractions.

# Curriculum Sequence

## Before This Unit

### Fractions and Decimals

In Units 3 and 5, students developed fraction concepts and skills using a variety of concrete models, including rectangles on dot paper. Students used concrete models to make connections between fractions and decimals in Unit 7. In Unit 7 Lesson 1, they used centiwheels to find decimal equivalents (or decimal approximations) for fractions.

## After This Unit

Students will explore multiplying fractions in Unit 12.

# Materials List

## Supplies and Copies

| Student | Teacher |
|---|---|
| **Supplies for Each Student**<br>• small centiwheel<br>• calculator | **Supplies** |
| **Copies**<br>• 1 wheel from *Small Centiwheels* per student, optional (*Unit Resource Guide* Page 38)<br>• 1 copy of *Centimeter Dot Paper* per student, optional (*Unit Resource Guide* Page 39) | **Copies/Transparencies**<br>• 1 copy of *Observational Assessment Record* to be used throughout this unit (*Unit Resource Guide* Pages 11–12) |

*All blackline masters including assessment, transparency, and DPP masters are also on the Teacher Resource CD.*

## Student Books

*Fractions and Division* (*Student Guide* Pages 286–293)
*Dividing Pizzas* (*Discovery Assignment Book* Pages 151–152)

## Daily Practice and Problems and Home Practice

DPP items A–D (*Unit Resource Guide* Pages 14–15)
Home Practice Part 1 (*Discovery Assignment Book* Page 147)

Note: Classrooms whose pacing differs significantly from the suggested pacing of the units should use the Math Facts Calendar in Section 4 of the *Facts Resource Guide* to ensure students receive the complete math facts program.

## Assessment Tools

*Observational Assessment Record* (*Unit Resource Guide* Pages 11–12)

# Daily Practice and Problems

Suggestions for using the DPPs are on page 35.

### A. Bit: Division Practice (URG p. 14) 

Use paper and pencil or mental math to solve the following problems. Estimate to be sure your answer is reasonable.

A. $678 \div 4 =$
B. $200 \div 5 =$
C. $56 \div 5 =$
D. $1264 \div 8 =$

### B. Task: Arrival Time (URG p. 14) 

Los Angeles is in the Pacific Standard Time (PST) zone and New York is in the Eastern Standard Time (EST) zone. When it is noon in Los Angeles, it is 3:00 P.M. in New York.

A plane leaves New York at 8:30 A.M. and takes 5 hours to fly to Los Angeles. The time in Los Angeles is always 3 hours earlier than New York. What time will the plane arrive in Los Angeles?

### C. Bit: Bargain Shopping (URG p. 15)   

Frank needs to buy school supplies. He needs four of each item. For each item, help Frank decide whether he will save money by buying the items in packs or individually. Figure out how much he will save on each item. Then, find his total savings.

| Item | Packs of 4 | Individual |
|---|---|---|
| pencils | 18¢ | 4¢ |
| rulers | 98¢ | 25¢ |
| folders | 45¢ | 12¢ |
| crayons | 29¢ | 7¢ |
| pens | $1.40 | 36¢ |

### D. Challenge: Arranging Colors (URG p. 15) 

Lee Yah received three different-colored sweatshirts for her birthday—blue, red, and yellow. She is deciding which one to wear to school on Monday, Tuesday, and Wednesday.

1. In what order can she wear the three sweatshirts? List all the different ways.
2. If Lee Yah decides to wear the blue sweatshirt on Monday, in what order can she wear the other two shirts? List all possibilities.
3. If she chooses not to wear the blue and yellow sweatshirts in a row (not blue, yellow and not yellow, blue), in what order could she wear the three sweatshirts? List all the different ways.

## Before the Activity

If students no longer have their small centiwheels, make new ones using the *Small Centiwheels* Activity Page in the Unit 7 Lesson 1 Lesson Guide.

## Teaching the Activity

### Part 1 Fractions and Division

Read the vignette on the *Fractions and Division* Activity Pages in the *Student Guide.* Students in small groups should discuss strategies for sharing 2 brownies among 3 boys. Encourage students to use various tools such as rectangles on dot paper or calculators.

***Question 1*** shows one strategy for dividing the brownies (see Figure 1). Note that we draw 3 × 4 rectangles on dot paper here. Students can also use 1 × 3 rectangles for this problem but a 3 × 4 rectangle will work for ***Question 2*** as well. There are other ways to divide the brownies.

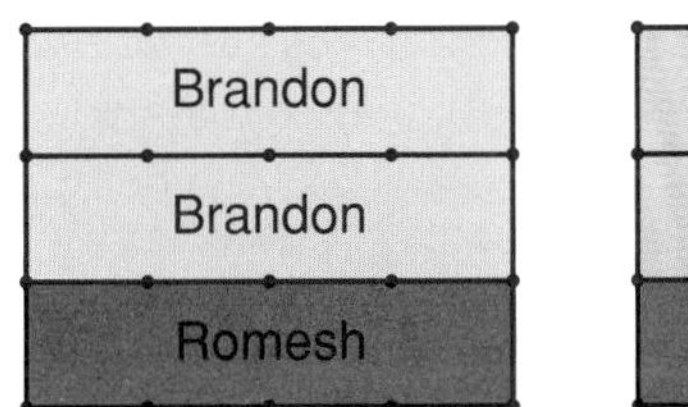


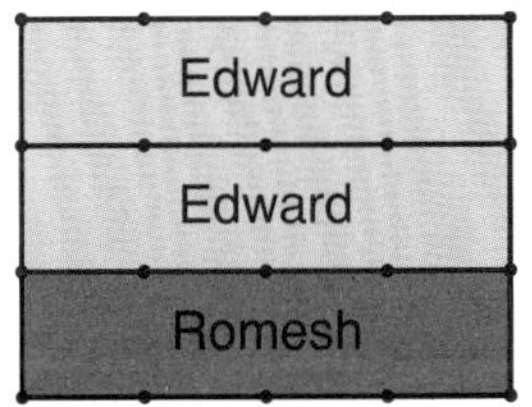


**Figure 1:** *Dividing two brownies among three boys—each boy gets $\frac{2}{3}$ of a brownie.*

***Question 2*** asks students to divide the two brownies among four boys and show their solutions in a drawing using two rectangles. (Drawing their rectangles on dot paper as they did in Unit 5 may be helpful or students may choose to simply sketch rectangles and show possible divisions.) A solution drawn on dot paper is shown in Figure 2. Discuss the fractions represented by the students' pictures.

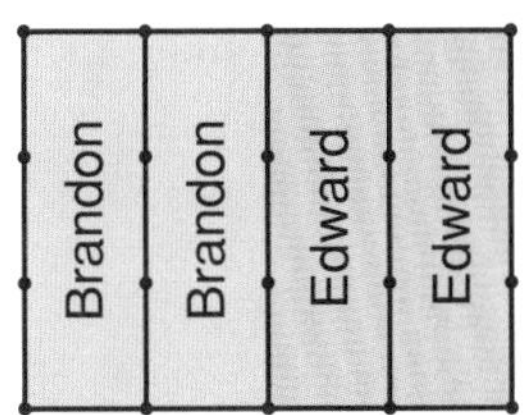


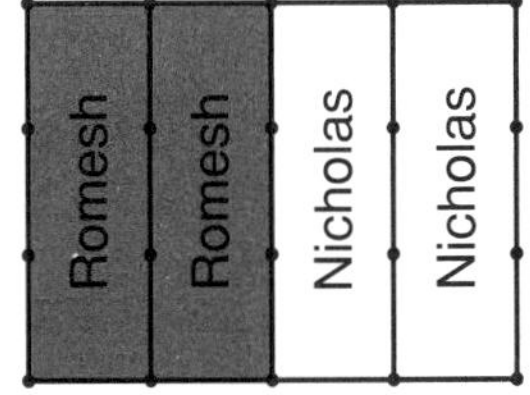


**Figure 2:** *Dividing two brownies among four boys—each boy gets $\frac{2}{4}$ of a brownie.*

Ask students to use rectangles to find other possible strategies to divide two brownies among four boys. Make sure students understand that the amount of

### Fractions and Division

Edward and Brandon walk into the lunch room. Edward says, "My mom packed 2 brownies in my lunch today. I'll share them with you if you want."

"Sure," Brandon replies. "We can each have one brownie then."

As the boys sit down, Romesh walks over and joins them. "Those brownies look great. How about sharing them with me, please?"

"Okay, but how can we share them equally?" Edward asks.

1. Think about how the three boys can share the two brownies equally. One solution is to divide each brownie into three equal pieces. You can show this using rectangles on dot paper.

Brandon / Brandon / Romesh — Edward / Edward / Romesh

A. How many pieces will each boy get?
B. What fraction of 1 whole brownie does this represent?



**Student Guide - page 286** *(Answers on p. 40)*

2. A. Nicholas joins the boys at their table. They decide to split the 2 brownies among the four boys. Draw rectangles to show how you can divide 2 brownies among the four boys.
   B. If they divide each brownie into four equal pieces, how many pieces will each boy get?
   C. What fraction of one whole brownie does this represent?
   D. Using rectangles, find another way to divide the two brownies among 4 boys.

A fraction is also a way to show division. The fraction line, or bar, means you divide the numerator by the denominator. For example, $\frac{2}{3}$ means 2 divided by 3. We can write this as a division number sentence:

$$\frac{2}{3} = 2 \div 3$$

The following chart shows what happens when 2 brownies are shared with more and more people.

Sharing Brownies

| Number of Brownies | Number of Boys | Number of Brownies Each Boy Will Get | Division Number Sentence |
|---|---|---|---|
| 2 | 1 | $\frac{2 \text{ brownies}}{1 \text{ boy}}$ = 2 brownies per boy | $2 \div 1 = 2$ |
| 2 | 2 | $\frac{2 \text{ brownies}}{2 \text{ boys}}$ = 1 brownie per boy | $2 \div 2 = 1$ |
| 2 | 3 | $\frac{2 \text{ brownies}}{3 \text{ boys}}$ = $\frac{2}{3}$ of a brownie per boy | $2 \div 3 = \frac{2}{3}$ |
| 2 | 4 | $\frac{2 \text{ brownies}}{4 \text{ boys}}$ = $\frac{2}{4}$ of a brownie per boy | $2 \div 4 = \frac{2}{4}$ |
| 2 | 5 | ? | ? |



**Student Guide - page 287** *(Answers on p. 40)*

3. A. If Edward divides his 2 brownies among 5 people, what fraction of a brownie will each person get?

B. Write the division number sentence that this fraction represents. Use the boxes as a guide.

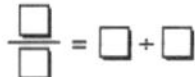

4. A. Brandon's mother packed 6 cookies in his lunch. How can Brandon share his six cookies with Edward, Romesh, and Nicholas? (*Note:* The 6 cookies will be divided among 4 boys.)

B. 6 cookies ÷ 4 boys = ? Draw circles to represent the 6 cookies. Show how Brandon can divide the cookies fairly among the 4 boys. How many will each of the four boys get?

C. What are other names for this number?

**Decimals**

We can use a calculator to change fractions to decimals.

5. Jackie shares her apple with Nila. If they share it fairly, how much apple will each girl get?

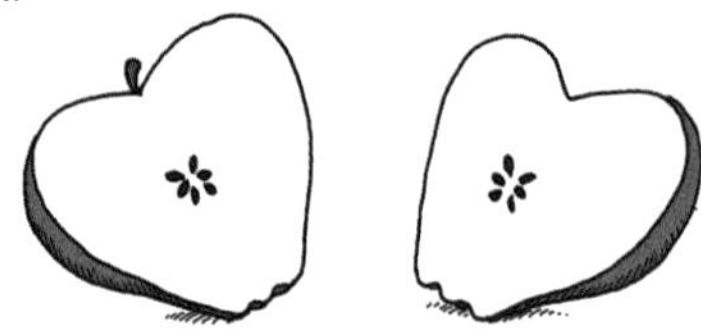

Each girl will get $\frac{1}{2}$ of the apple. This fraction means 1 apple divided between 2 girls or 1 ÷ 2. Use your calculator to find a decimal equivalent to $\frac{1}{2}$ by pressing [1] [÷] [2] [=]. You should see 0.5 on your calculator. This tells you that 0.5 is equal to $\frac{1}{2}$. Notice that $\frac{1}{2} + \frac{1}{2} = 1$ just as 0.5 + 0.5 = 1.

288 SG • Grade 5 • Unit 9 • Lesson 1 Fractions and Division

***Student Guide* - page 288** *(Answers on p. 41)*

Some students may still need to use drawings of rectangles to show the division problem in ***Question 3***. Encourage students to use this strategy as needed.

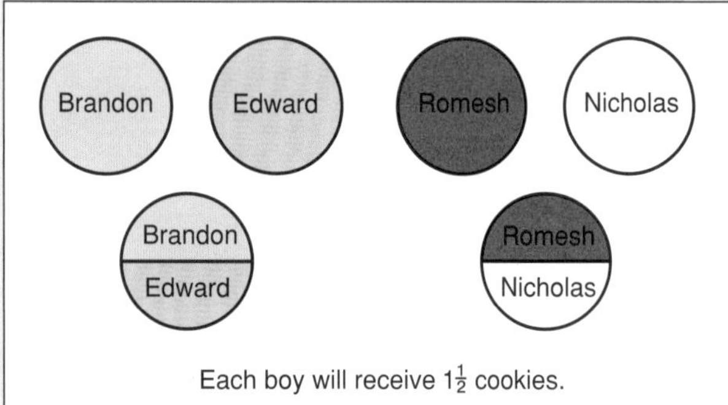


**Figure 4:** *Dividing six cookies among four boys*

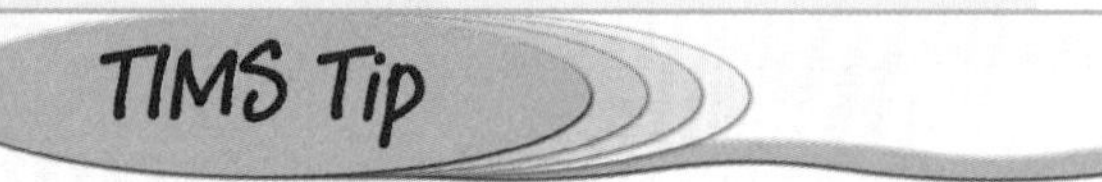


Students should use the division key on their calculators that results in decimal answers and not use integer division.

brownie each boy receives will not change, but the fraction name may change. For example, $\frac{2}{4}$ of a brownie is the same as $\frac{1}{2}$ the brownie.

Ask students how the four boys can divide the brownies evenly if they have already cut them into three pieces as shown in ***Question 1.*** One solution is to give each boy $\frac{2}{6} + \frac{1}{6}$ of a brownie as shown in Figure 3.

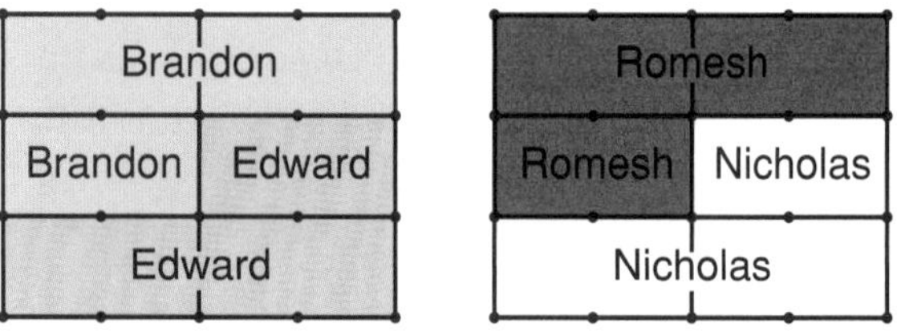


**Figure 3:** *Each of the 4 boys gets $\frac{2}{6} + \frac{1}{6}$ or $\frac{1}{2}$ of a brownie.*

After discussing these two questions, connect fractions to division. Ask:

- *Which operation did the boys use to share the brownies: addition, subtraction, multiplication, or division?* (Students should realize that the boys were dividing. Explain that the line between the numerator and the denominator means you can divide the numerator by the denominator.)

Students use the Sharing Brownies data table to answer ***Question 3.*** If you divide 2 brownies among 5 people, each person will get $\frac{2}{5}$ of a brownie. We can write the following division number sentence: $2 \div 5 = \frac{2}{5}$.

In ***Question 4,*** students divide six cookies among four boys. They can draw circles to represent the cookies. Ask them to explore the different ways they can divide these cookies. One possible way is shown in Figure 4. Alternatively, they can use division to solve the problem.

$$\frac{6 \text{ cookies}}{4 \text{ boys}} \text{ or } 6 \div 4 = \frac{6}{4}$$

Discuss the division with students. They should find that each boy will receive $1\frac{1}{2}$ cookies. They also should recognize different names for $1\frac{1}{2}$, including $\frac{3}{2}$ and $\frac{6}{4}$ and 1.5.

Once students understand these concepts, assign the *Dividing Pizzas* Homework Pages in the *Discovery Assignment Book.*

**Part 2 Decimals**

Students use the Decimals section of the *Fractions and Division* Activity Pages in the *Student Guide* for this part of the lesson. Each student will need a small centiwheel and calculator to complete this section.

In the first part of ***Question 5,*** students should recognize that if 2 girls split 1 apple, each girl gets $\frac{1}{2}$ the apple. Students then use division on their calculators to find a decimal equivalent for $\frac{1}{2}$ ($1 \div 2 = 0.5$).

***Question 6*** gives students further practice with tenths. Students draw a picture showing how to divide four granola bars equally among five children. See Figure 5 for one solution. They are then asked to use a calculator to find the decimal equivalent for this fraction. Check to be sure students are using their calculators correctly. They should be able to read 0.8 (eight-tenths) accurately and connect 0.8 to $\frac{4}{5}$. Point out that $0.8 + 0.8 + 0.8 + 0.8 + 0.8$ or $0.8 \times 5 = 4$ on the calculator.

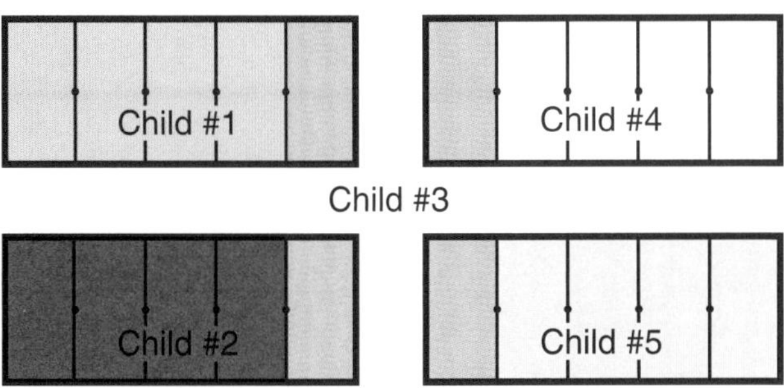


Each child will receive $\frac{4}{5}$ or 0.8 of a granola bar.

**Figure 5:** *Dividing four granola bars among five children*

Four boys share one pizza in ***Question 7.*** Students should recognize that each boy will receive $\frac{1}{4}$ of the pizza. Ask students to find the decimal equivalent for $\frac{1}{4}$. Using what they learned in Unit 7, many students will recognize that $\frac{1}{4} = 0.25$ without using their calculators.

***Question 8*** asks students to use a calculator to find the decimal equivalent for $\frac{1}{8}$. Make sure students can read the 0.125 accurately as one hundred twenty-five thousandths.

Students can complete ***Questions 9–10*** with a partner. Each student should complete the calculator work independently and then compare his or her results with the partner's before proceeding. Take some time to explore the relationship between the fractions and their decimal equivalents. For example, $\frac{3}{4}$ is the same as $3 \times \frac{1}{4}$ and 0.75 is the same as $3 \times 0.25$.

Encourage students to make connections between the fractions and their decimal equivalents. They can make visual representations using centiwheels. They can also connect the decimals to money. For example, a quarter ($\frac{1}{4}$) of a dollar is \$0.25.

6. A. Felicia has 4 granola bars to share among 5 children. Use rectangles to show how Felicia can divide the four granola bars among 5 people.
   B. What fraction of one granola bar will each child get?
   C. Use your calculator to find the decimal equivalent. What are other names for this number?
   D. Complete this number sentence: $0.8 = \frac{?}{5}$
7. A. Frank, Roberto, Michael, and Manny share one pizza. What fraction of the pizza will each boy get?
   B. Use your calculator to find the decimal equivalent.
   C. What are other names for this number?
8. A. Shannon's mother baked a pie. She cut the pie into 8 equal pieces. Each piece is what fraction of the pie?
   B. Use your calculator to find a decimal for this fraction.
   C. What are other names for this number?
   D. Complete the following number sentence: $\frac{1}{8} = \frac{?}{1000}$

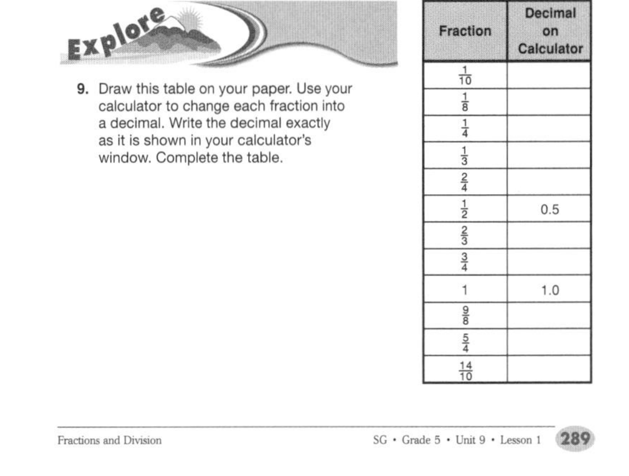


9. Draw this table on your paper. Use your calculator to change each fraction into a decimal. Write the decimal exactly as it is shown in your calculator's window. Complete the table.

| Fraction | Decimal on Calculator |
|---|---|
| $\frac{1}{10}$ | |
| $\frac{1}{8}$ | |
| $\frac{1}{4}$ | |
| $\frac{1}{3}$ | |
| $\frac{2}{4}$ | |
| $\frac{1}{2}$ | 0.5 |
| $\frac{2}{3}$ | |
| $\frac{3}{4}$ | |
| 1 | 1.0 |
| $\frac{9}{8}$ | |
| $\frac{5}{4}$ | |
| $\frac{14}{10}$ | |

Fractions and Division SG • Grade 5 • Unit 9 • Lesson 1 289

***Student Guide* - page 289** *(Answers on p. 41)*

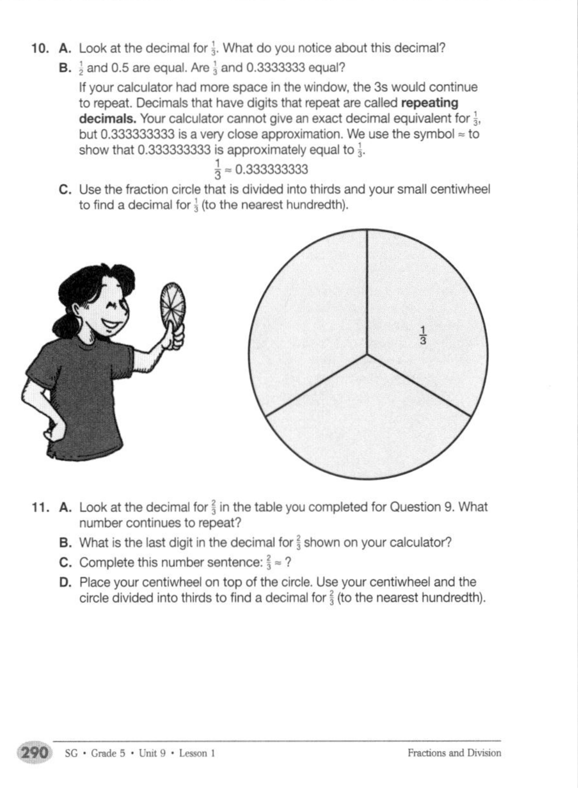

10. A. Look at the decimal for $\frac{1}{3}$. What do you notice about this decimal?
    B. $\frac{1}{2}$ and 0.5 are equal. Are $\frac{1}{3}$ and 0.3333333 equal?
    If your calculator had more space in the window, the 3s would continue to repeat. Decimals that have digits that repeat are called **repeating decimals.** Your calculator cannot give an exact decimal equivalent for $\frac{1}{3}$, but 0.333333333 is a very close approximation. We use the symbol ≈ to show that 0.333333333 is approximately equal to $\frac{1}{3}$.
    $$\frac{1}{3} \approx 0.333333333$$
    C. Use the fraction circle that is divided into thirds and your small centiwheel to find a decimal for $\frac{1}{3}$ (to the nearest hundredth).



11. A. Look at the decimal for $\frac{2}{3}$ in the table you completed for Question 9. What number continues to repeat?
    B. What is the last digit in the decimal for $\frac{2}{3}$ shown on your calculator?
    C. Complete this number sentence: $\frac{2}{3} \approx$ ?
    D. Place your centiwheel on top of the circle. Use your centiwheel and the circle divided into thirds to find a decimal for $\frac{2}{3}$ (to the nearest hundredth).

290 SG • Grade 5 • Unit 9 • Lesson 1 Fractions and Division

***Student Guide* - page 290** *(Answers on p. 42)*

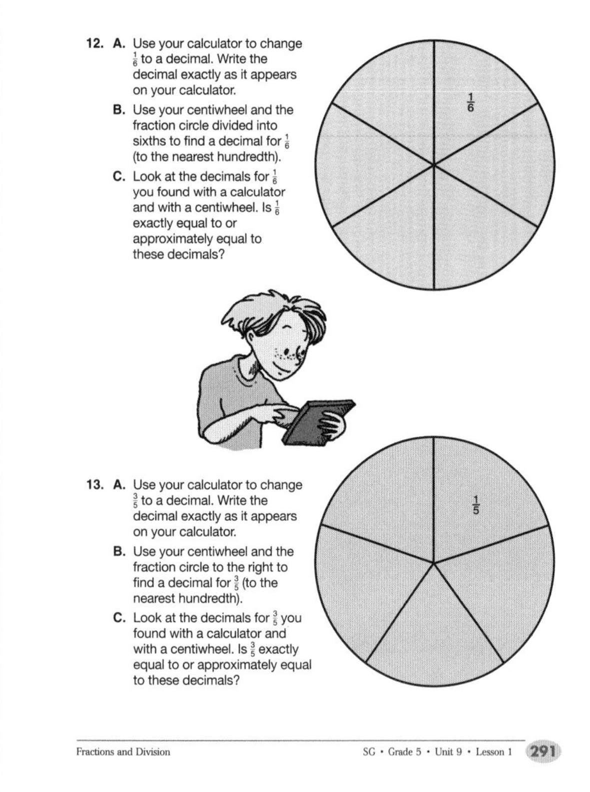

12. A. Use your calculator to change $\frac{1}{6}$ to a decimal. Write the decimal exactly as it appears on your calculator.
    B. Use your centiwheel and the fraction circle divided into sixths to find a decimal for $\frac{1}{6}$ (to the nearest hundredth).
    C. Look at the decimals for $\frac{1}{6}$ you found with a calculator and with a centiwheel. Is $\frac{1}{6}$ exactly equal to or approximately equal to these decimals?

13. A. Use your calculator to change $\frac{3}{5}$ to a decimal. Write the decimal exactly as it appears on your calculator.
    B. Use your centiwheel and the fraction circle to the right to find a decimal for $\frac{3}{5}$ (to the nearest hundredth).
    C. Look at the decimals for $\frac{3}{5}$ you found with a calculator and with a centiwheel. Is $\frac{3}{5}$ exactly equal to or approximately equal to these decimals?



Fractions and Division SG • Grade 5 • Unit 9 • Lesson 1 291

***Student Guide* - page 291** *(Answers on p. 42)*

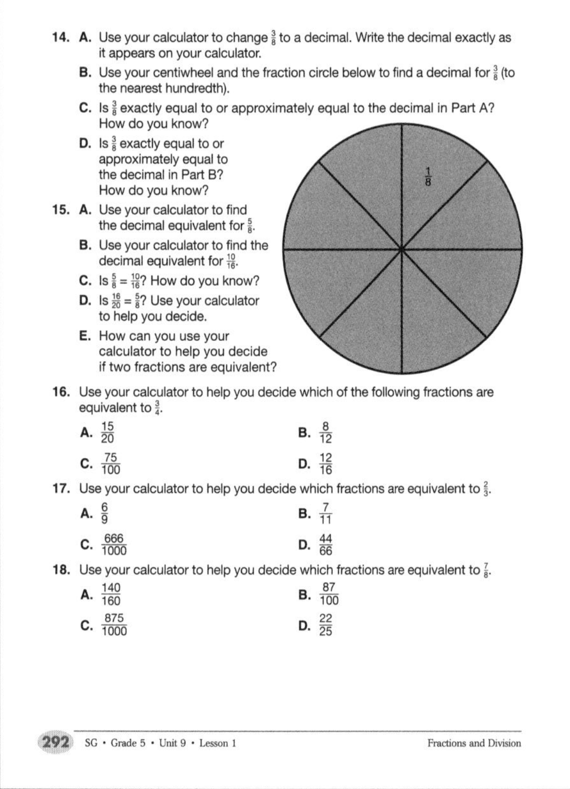

14. A. Use your calculator to change $\frac{3}{8}$ to a decimal. Write the decimal exactly as it appears on your calculator.
    B. Use your centiwheel and the fraction circle below to find a decimal for $\frac{3}{8}$ (to the nearest hundredth).
    C. Is $\frac{3}{8}$ exactly equal to or approximately equal to the decimal in Part A? How do you know?
    D. Is $\frac{3}{8}$ exactly equal to or approximately equal to the decimal in Part B? How do you know?
15. A. Use your calculator to find the decimal equivalent for $\frac{5}{8}$.
    B. Use your calculator to find the decimal equivalent for $\frac{10}{16}$.
    C. Is $\frac{5}{8} = \frac{10}{16}$? How do you know?
    D. Is $\frac{16}{20} = \frac{5}{8}$? Use your calculator to help you decide.
    E. How can you use your calculator to help you decide if two fractions are equivalent?
16. Use your calculator to help you decide which of the following fractions are equivalent to $\frac{3}{4}$.
    A. $\frac{15}{20}$ B. $\frac{8}{12}$
    C. $\frac{75}{100}$ D. $\frac{12}{16}$
17. Use your calculator to help you decide which fractions are equivalent to $\frac{2}{3}$.
    A. $\frac{6}{9}$ B. $\frac{7}{11}$
    C. $\frac{666}{1000}$ D. $\frac{44}{66}$
18. Use your calculator to help you decide which fractions are equivalent to $\frac{7}{8}$.
    A. $\frac{140}{160}$ B. $\frac{87}{100}$
    C. $\frac{875}{1000}$ D. $\frac{22}{25}$



292 SG • Grade 5 • Unit 9 • Lesson 1 Fractions and Division

***Student Guide* - page 292** *(Answers on p. 43)*

Students will need small centiwheels to complete ***Questions 10–14.*** You may need to review how to use a centiwheel to find a decimal (or decimal approximation) for a fraction. Figure 6 shows how to find a decimal approximation for $\frac{1}{3}$ using a centiwheel. Point out to students that 0.33 is just an approximation since the line for $\frac{1}{3}$ lies between $\frac{33}{100}$ and $\frac{34}{100}$ on the wheel.

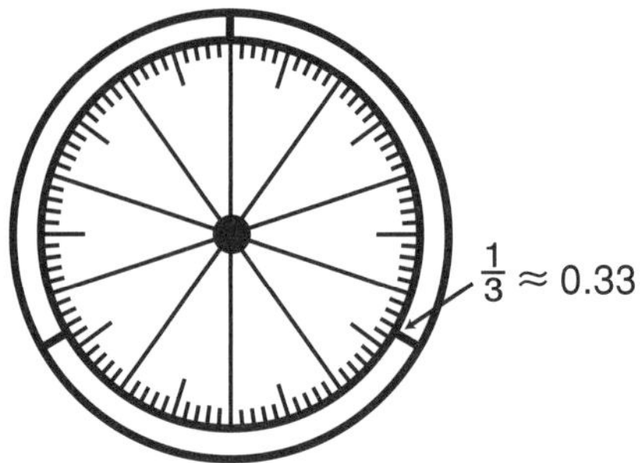



**Figure 6:** *Decimal approximation for $\frac{1}{3}$ using a centiwheel*

Discuss repeating decimals ***(Question 10).*** To help illustrate that 0.3333333 is approximately equal to $\frac{1}{3}$, ask students to multiply 0.3333333 by 3 by directly entering: 0.3333333 × 3 = . Students will note that the answer is 0.9999999. Explain that this is very close to 1, since1 – 0.9999999 = 0.0000001.

## Content Note

Most calculators display 8 digits (or more) in their window. When an answer results in more than 8 digits, the calculator stores several additional digits in its memory and rounds the answer to 8 digits. For example, if you ask students to find the answer to $\frac{1}{3} \times 3$ on their calculator, the answer displayed with be 1, rather than 0.9999999. Why does that happen? Because after typing 1 ÷ 3 × the window will show 0.3333333 (eight digits), but the memory of the calculator will actually contain 0.333333333 (10 digits). Then, if you enter 3 =, the calculator will round off the answer, 0.999999999 to eight digits, which is 1.

Students continue to work with their partners to complete ***Questions 11–14.*** They use calculators and centiwheels to find decimal equivalents or decimal approximations for fractions. Students are asked which of the decimals are decimal equivalents and which are approximations. If the decimal has repeating digits that fill the calculator display ($\frac{2}{3}$ = 0.666666667), we can be fairly certain the digits will continue to repeat and that the decimal in the display is an approximation. If the decimal terminates ($\frac{1}{8}$ = 0.125), then we know the decimal is equal to the fraction.

***Questions 15–18*** guide students toward a strategy for using calculators to see if two fractions are equivalent. They can use a calculator to find a decimal for each fraction. Then if both decimals are equivalent, the fractions are equivalent. Point out ***Question 17C*** to students. Here $\frac{666}{1000} = 0.666$ which, although close to $\frac{2}{3}$, is not equivalent to $\frac{2}{3}$.

What are some advantages to expressing fractions as decimals?

## Homework and Practice

- Assign the *Dividing Pizzas* Homework Pages in the *Discovery Assignment Book* after completing ***Question 4*** (Part 1) in the *Student Guide.* Students should draw pictures when needed.
- Assign ***Questions 1–5*** in the Homework section of the *Student Guide* after completing the lesson. Students will need a calculator and a small centiwheel to complete this work.
- Assign DPP items A–D for further practice with computation, elapsed time, and problem solving.
- Assign Part 1 of the Home Practice that practices division.

*Answers for Part 1 of the Home Practice are in the Answer Key at the end of this lesson and at the end of this unit.*

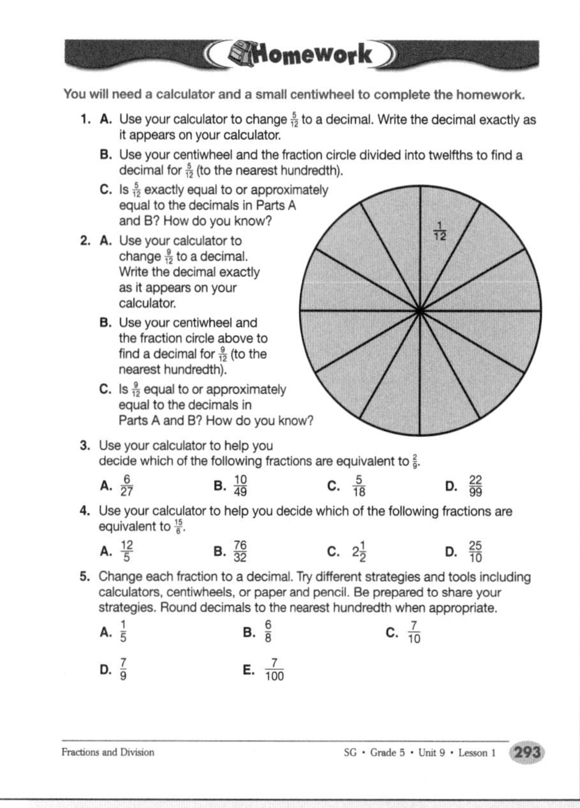

### Homework

**You will need a calculator and a small centiwheel to complete the homework.**

1. **A.** Use your calculator to change $\frac{5}{12}$ to a decimal. Write the decimal exactly as it appears on your calculator.
   **B.** Use your centiwheel and the fraction circle divided into twelfths to find a decimal for $\frac{5}{12}$ (to the nearest hundredth).
   **C.** Is $\frac{5}{12}$ exactly equal to or approximately equal to the decimals in Parts A and B? How do you know?
2. **A.** Use your calculator to change $\frac{9}{12}$ to a decimal. Write the decimal exactly as it appears on your calculator.
   **B.** Use your centiwheel and the fraction circle above to find a decimal for $\frac{9}{12}$ (to the nearest hundredth).
   **C.** Is $\frac{9}{12}$ equal to or approximately equal to the decimals in Parts A and B? How do you know?
3. Use your calculator to help you decide which of the following fractions are equivalent to $\frac{2}{9}$.
   **A.** $\frac{6}{27}$ **B.** $\frac{10}{49}$ **C.** $\frac{5}{18}$ **D.** $\frac{22}{99}$
4. Use your calculator to help you decide which of the following fractions are equivalent to $\frac{15}{6}$.
   **A.** $\frac{12}{5}$ **B.** $\frac{76}{32}$ **C.** $2\frac{1}{2}$ **D.** $\frac{25}{10}$
5. Change each fraction to a decimal. Try different strategies and tools including calculators, centiwheels, or paper and pencil. Be prepared to share your strategies. Round decimals to the nearest hundredth when appropriate.
   **A.** $\frac{1}{5}$ **B.** $\frac{6}{8}$ **C.** $\frac{7}{10}$
   **D.** $\frac{7}{9}$ **E.** $\frac{7}{100}$

$\frac{1}{12}$

Fractions and Division SG • Grade 5 • Unit 9 • Lesson 1 293

***Student Guide* - page 293** *(Answers on p. 44)*

Name ______________________ Date ______________

## Unit 9 Home Practice

**PART 1 Division Practice**

**Solve each problem using paper and pencil. Estimate to see if your answers are reasonable. Explain your estimation strategy for Question A.**

A. 5762 ÷ 8 = B. 1263 ÷ 9 =

C. 4691 ÷ 3 = D. 3189 ÷ 3 =

**PART 2 Fractions and Decimals**

1. Find a pair of equivalent fractions in each set. You may use a calculator or another strategy. Be prepared to explain your thinking.

| | | | | |
|---|---|---|---|---|
| A. | $\frac{7}{15}$ | $\frac{28}{75}$ | $\frac{79}{160}$ | $\frac{21}{45}$ |
| B. | $\frac{15}{20}$ | $\frac{125}{200}$ | $\frac{3}{5}$ | $\frac{27}{45}$ |
| C. | $\frac{1}{3}$ | $\frac{33}{100}$ | $\frac{4}{5}$ | $\frac{11}{33}$ |
| D. | $\frac{6}{16}$ | $\frac{24}{36}$ | $\frac{36}{112}$ | $\frac{66}{176}$ |

2. Use your calculator to change each fraction to a decimal (to the nearest hundredth). Then change each decimal to a percent.

| | Decimal | Percent |
|---|---|---|
| A. $\frac{4}{5}$ | ________ | ________ |
| B. $\frac{7}{12}$ | ________ | ________ |
| C. $\frac{4}{15}$ | ________ | ________ |



CONNECTIONS TO DIVISION DAB • Grade 5 • Unit 9 147

***Discovery Assignment Book* - page 147** *(Answers on p. 45)*

Name ______________________ Date ______________

## Dividing Pizzas

1. Lin is planning a sleep-over. Her mother says she can invite 3 girls to spend the night so there will be 4 girls in all. Lin wants to order pizzas, but is not sure how many to order. Answer the following questions. Draw a picture when it helps.

   A. If Lin orders one pizza and the girls split it evenly, what fraction of the pizza will each of the girls get?

   B. Write the division number sentence that this fraction represents. Use the boxes as a guide.

   $\square \div \square = \frac{\square}{\square}$

2. A. If Lin orders three pizzas and the girls split them fairly, what fraction of one pizza will each girl get?

   B. Write the division number sentence that this fraction represents. Use the boxes as a guide.

   $\square \div \square = \frac{\square}{\square}$



Fractions and Division DAB • Grade 5 • Unit 9 • Lesson 1 151

***Discovery Assignment Book* - page 151** *(Answers on p. 45)*

Name ______________________ Date ______________

3. The table below shows what happens when you share four pizzas with more and more people. Complete each column. Draw pictures when it helps.

Sharing Pizzas

| Number of Pizzas | Number of People | Number of Pizzas Each Person Will Get | Division Number Sentence |
|---|---|---|---|
| 4 | 1 | | |
| 4 | 2 | | 4 ÷ 2 = 2 |
| 4 | 3 | | |
| 4 | 4 | $\frac{4 \text{ pizzas}}{4 \text{ people}}$ = 1 pizza per person | |
| 4 | 5 | | |
| 4 | 10 | | |
| 4 | 20 | | |

4. Look at the chart. Describe the patterns you see.



152 DAB • Grade 5 • Unit 9 • Lesson 1 Fractions and Division

***Discovery Assignment Book* - page 152** *(Answers on p. 46)*

## Assessment

You can use the homework activities as assessments. Select specific questions to evaluate students' work. Use ***Question 3*** on the *Dividing Pizzas* Homework Pages in the *Discovery Assignment Book* to assess students' abilities to see patterns with fractions. Use Homework ***Questions 2–4*** in the *Student Guide* to assess students' abilities to change fractions to decimal fractions for comparison. Use the *Observational Assessment Record* to note students' abilities to find decimal equivalents for fractions.

## Literature Connection

*Little House in the Big Woods,* by Laura Ingalls Wilder, HarperCollins, New York, 2001. In Chapter 10, "Summertime," Ma lets Laura and Mary go to visit Mrs. Peterson. Mrs. Peterson gives each girl 1 cookie. They decide to save some for Baby Carrie, so they each eat $\frac{1}{2}$ of their cookie. When they get home, they realize that with their 2 halves, Baby Carrie gets a whole cookie. While they know this is not quite fair, they can't decide how to divide the two cookies equally among the three children.

After reading this selection to your class, suggest that students use rectangles or circles to decide how to divide the two cookies evenly among the 3 girls.

Estimated Class Sessions

**2**

# At a Glance

## Math Facts and Daily Practice and Problems

DPP items A–D review division, elapsed time, and problem solving.

## Part 1. Fractions and Division

1. Read and discuss the vignette in the *Student Guide*.
2. Use ***Questions 1–4*** to connect fractions and division.

## Part 2. Decimals

1. Use ***Questions 5–8*** to show students how to use calculators to find decimal equivalents for fractions.
2. Students work in pairs to change fractions to decimals using calculators. ***(Question 9)***
3. Students use calculators and centiwheels to find approximations for repeating decimals and equivalents for terminating decimals. ***(Questions 10–14)***
4. Students learn to use calculators to compare fractions to see if they are equivalent. ***(Questions 15–18)***

## Homework

1. Assign the *Dividing Pizzas* Homework Pages in the *Discovery Assignment Book* after Part 1 of the lesson.
2. Assign the Homework section in the *Student Guide*.
3. Assign Part 1 of the Home Practice.

## Assessment

1. Use some of the questions on the homework pages as assessments. ***Question 3*** on the *Dividing Pizzas* Homework Pages and ***Questions 2–4*** in the *Student Guide* Homework section are good choices.
2. Use the *Observational Assessment Record* to note students' abilities to find decimal equivalents for fractions.

## Connection

Read a section of *Little House in the Big Woods* to your class and discuss how to divide two cookies among three girls.

*Answer Key is on pages 40–46.*

## Notes:

Name ______________________________ Date ______________

# Small Centiwheels

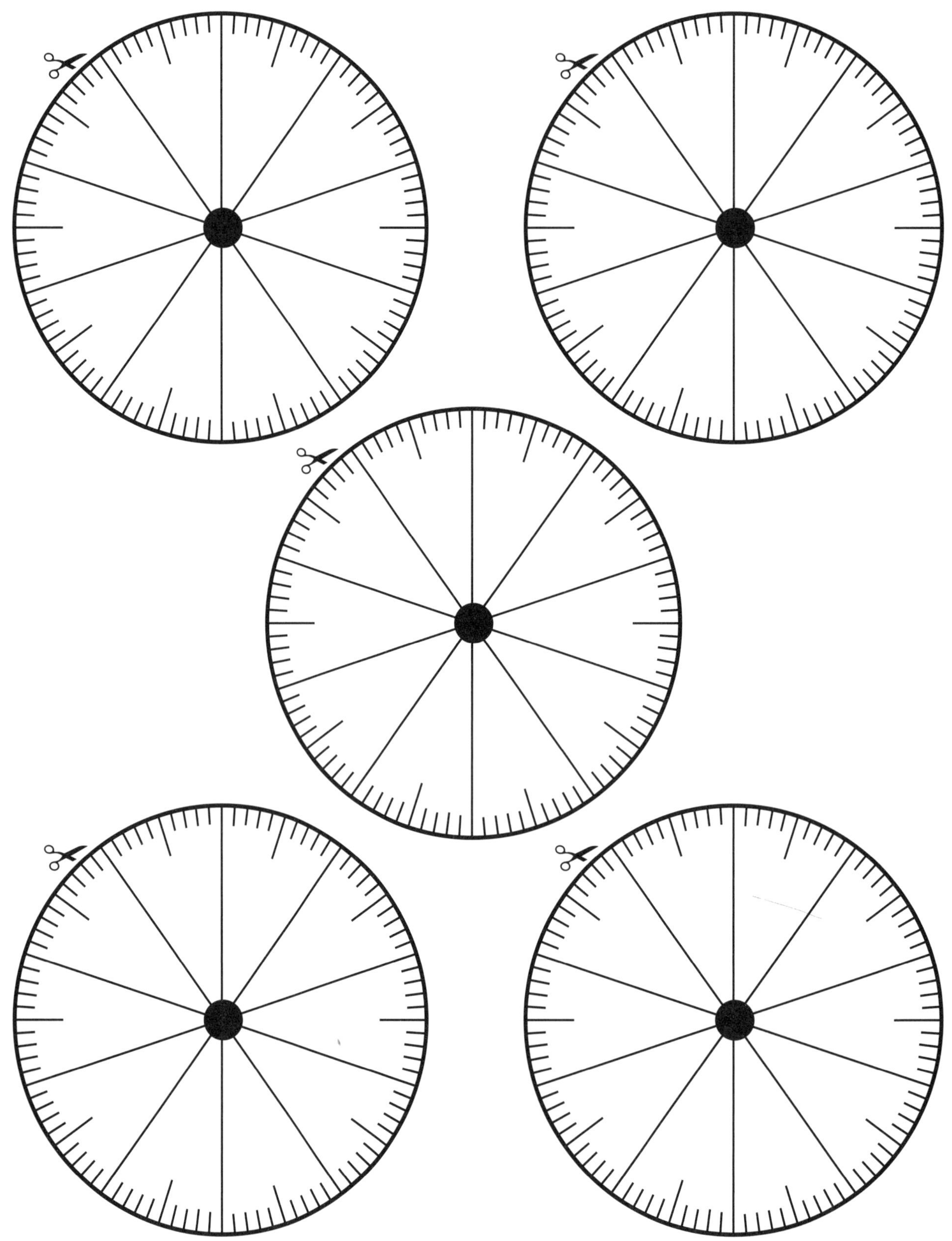

Name ______________________ Date ____________

# Centimeter Dot Paper

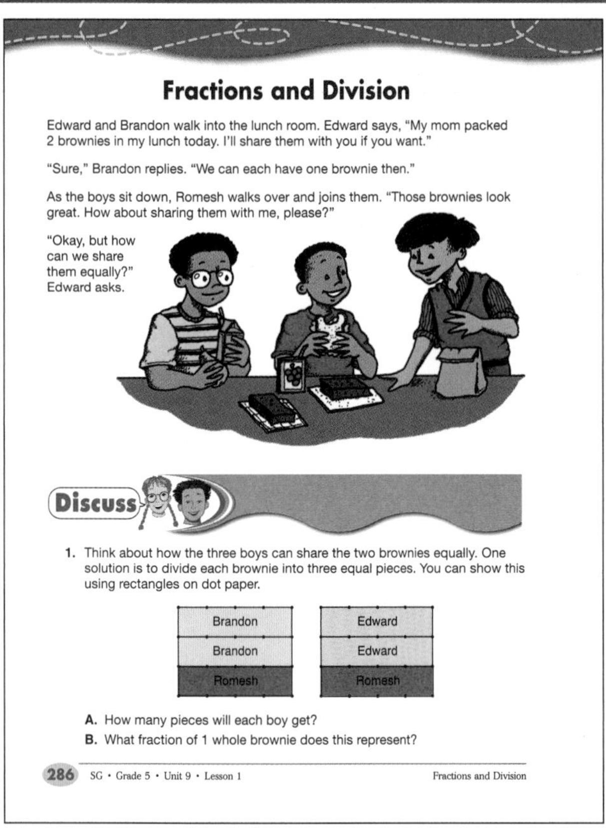

## Fractions and Division

Edward and Brandon walk into the lunch room. Edward says, "My mom packed 2 brownies in my lunch today. I'll share them with you if you want."

"Sure," Brandon replies. "We can each have one brownie then."

As the boys sit down, Romesh walks over and joins them. "Those brownies look great. How about sharing them with me, please?"

"Okay, but how can we share them equally?" Edward asks.

Discuss

1. Think about how the three boys can share the two brownies equally. One solution is to divide each brownie into three equal pieces. You can show this using rectangles on dot paper.

| Brandon | Edward |
|---|---|
| Brandon | Edward |
| Romesh | Romesh |

A. How many pieces will each boy get?
B. What fraction of 1 whole brownie does this represent?

286 SG • Grade 5 • Unit 9 • Lesson 1 Fractions and Division

***Student Guide* - page 286**

## Student Guide (p. 286)

### Fractions and Division

1. **A.** 2; See Figure 1 in Lesson Guide 1.
   **B.** $\frac{2}{3}$

2. **A.** Nicholas joins the boys at their table. They decide to split the 2 brownies among the four boys. Draw rectangles to show how you can divide 2 brownies among the four boys.
   **B.** If they divide each brownie into four equal pieces, how many pieces will each boy get?
   **C.** What fraction of one whole brownie does this represent?
   **D.** Using rectangles, find another way to divide the two brownies among 4 boys.

A fraction is also a way to show division. The fraction line, or bar, means you divide the numerator by the denominator. For example, $\frac{2}{3}$ means 2 divided by 3. We can write this as a division number sentence:

$$\frac{2}{3} = 2 \div 3$$

The following chart shows what happens when 2 brownies are shared with more and more people.

Sharing Brownies

| Number of Brownies | Number of Boys | Number of Brownies Each Boy Will Get | Division Number Sentence |
|---|---|---|---|
| 2 | 1 | $\frac{2 \text{ brownies}}{1 \text{ boy}}$ = 2 brownies per boy | $2 \div 1 = 2$ |
| 2 | 2 | $\frac{2 \text{ brownies}}{2 \text{ boys}}$ = 1 brownie per boy | $2 \div 2 = 1$ |
| 2 | 3 | $\frac{2 \text{ brownies}}{3 \text{ boys}}$ = $\frac{2}{3}$ of a brownie per boy | $2 \div 3 = \frac{2}{3}$ |
| 2 | 4 | $\frac{2 \text{ brownies}}{4 \text{ boys}}$ = $\frac{2}{4}$ of a brownie per boy | $2 \div 4 = \frac{2}{4}$ |
| 2 | 5 | ? | ? |

Fractions and Division SG • Grade 5 • Unit 9 • Lesson 1 287

***Student Guide* - page 287**

## Student Guide (p. 287)

2. **A.** See Figure 2 in Lesson Guide 1.*
   **B.** 2
   **C.** $\frac{2}{4} = \frac{1}{2}$
   **D.** See Figure 3 in Lesson Guide 1.*

*Answers and/or discussion are included in the Lesson Guide.

## Student Guide (pp. 288–289)

3. A. $\frac{2}{5}$*
   B. $\frac{2}{5} = 2 \div 5$
4. A. $\frac{6}{4} = 1\frac{2}{4} = 1\frac{1}{2}$*
   B. See Figure 4 in Lesson Guide 1.*
   C. $\frac{3}{2}$ and any number equivalent to $\frac{3}{2}$
5. $\frac{1}{2}$*
6. A. See Figure 5 in Lesson Guide 1.*
   B. $\frac{4}{5}$
   C. 0.8; $\frac{8}{10}$ and any number equivalent to $\frac{4}{5}$
   D. $0.8 = \frac{4}{5}$
7. A. $\frac{1}{4}$*
   B. 0.25*
   C. $\frac{25}{100}$ and any number equivalent to $\frac{1}{4}$
8. A. $\frac{1}{8}$*
   B. 0.125*
   C. $\frac{125}{1000}$ and any number equivalent to 0.125
   D. $\frac{1}{8} = \frac{125}{1000}$
9. Answers will depend on calculator.

| Fraction | Decimal |
|---|---|
| $\frac{1}{10}$ | 0.1 |
| $\frac{1}{8}$ | 0.125 |
| $\frac{1}{4}$ | .25 |
| $\frac{1}{3}$ | 0.3333333 |
| $\frac{2}{4}$ | 0.5 |
| $\frac{1}{2}$ | 0.5 |
| $\frac{2}{3}$ | 0.6666667 |
| $\frac{3}{4}$ | 0.75 |
| 1 | 1.0 |
| $\frac{9}{8}$ | 1.125 |
| $\frac{5}{4}$ | 1.25 |
| $\frac{14}{10}$ | 1.4 |

3. A. If Edward divides his 2 brownies among 5 people, what fraction of a brownie will each person get?
   B. Write the division number sentence that this fraction represents. Use the boxes as a guide.

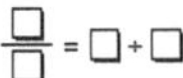

4. A. Brandon's mother packed 6 cookies in his lunch. How can Brandon share his six cookies with Edward, Romesh, and Nicholas? (*Note:* The 6 cookies will be divided among 4 boys.)
   B. 6 cookies ÷ 4 boys = ? Draw circles to represent the 6 cookies. Show how Brandon can divide the cookies fairly among the 4 boys. How many will each of the four boys get?
   C. What are other names for this number?

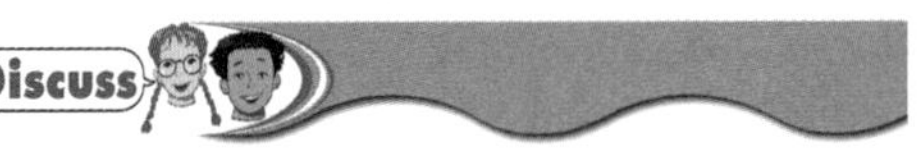


**Decimals**

We can use a calculator to change fractions to decimals.

5. Jackie shares her apple with Nila. If they share it fairly, how much apple will each girl get?

Each girl will get $\frac{1}{2}$ of the apple. This fraction means 1 apple divided between 2 girls or 1 ÷ 2. Use your calculator to find a decimal equivalent to $\frac{1}{2}$ by pressing [1] [÷] [2] [=]. You should see 0.5 on your calculator. This tells you that 0.5 is equal to $\frac{1}{2}$. Notice that $\frac{1}{2} + \frac{1}{2} = 1$ just as 0.5 + 0.5 = 1.

***Student Guide* - page 288**

6. A. Felicia has 4 granola bars to share among 5 children. Use rectangles to show how Felicia can divide the four granola bars among 5 people.
   B. What fraction of one granola bar will each child get?
   C. Use your calculator to find the decimal equivalent. What are other names for this number?
   D. Complete this number sentence: $0.8 = \frac{?}{5}$
7. A. Frank, Roberto, Michael, and Manny share one pizza. What fraction of the pizza will each boy get?
   B. Use your calculator to find the decimal equivalent.
   C. What are other names for this number?
8. A. Shannon's mother baked a pie. She cut the pie into 8 equal pieces. Each piece is what fraction of the pie?
   B. Use your calculator to find a decimal for this fraction.
   C. What are other names for this number?
   D. Complete the following number sentence: $\frac{1}{8} = \frac{?}{1000}$

Explore

9. Draw this table on your paper. Use your calculator to change each fraction into a decimal. Write the decimal exactly as it is shown in your calculator's window. Complete the table.

| Fraction | Decimal on Calculator |
|---|---|
| $\frac{1}{10}$ | |
| $\frac{1}{8}$ | |
| $\frac{1}{4}$ | |
| $\frac{1}{3}$ | |
| $\frac{2}{4}$ | |
| $\frac{1}{2}$ | 0.5 |
| $\frac{2}{3}$ | |
| $\frac{3}{4}$ | |
| 1 | 1.0 |
| $\frac{9}{8}$ | |
| $\frac{5}{4}$ | |
| $\frac{14}{10}$ | |



***Student Guide* - page 289**

*Answers and/or discussion are included in the Lesson Guide.

10. A. Look at the decimal for $\frac{1}{3}$. What do you notice about this decimal?

B. $\frac{1}{2}$ and 0.5 are equal. Are $\frac{1}{3}$ and 0.3333333 equal?

If your calculator had more space in the window, the 3s would continue to repeat. Decimals that have digits that repeat are called **repeating decimals.** Your calculator cannot give an exact decimal equivalent for $\frac{1}{3}$, but 0.333333333 is a very close approximation. We use the symbol ≈ to show that 0.333333333 is approximately equal to $\frac{1}{3}$.

$$\frac{1}{3} \approx 0.333333333$$

C. Use the fraction circle that is divided into thirds and your small centiwheel to find a decimal for $\frac{1}{3}$ (to the nearest hundredth).

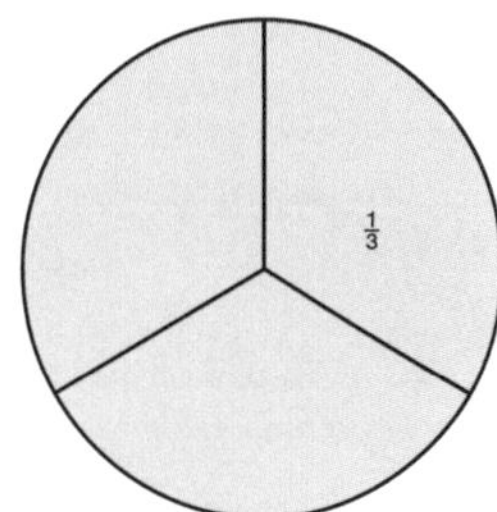

11. A. Look at the decimal for $\frac{2}{3}$ in the table you completed for Question 9. What number continues to repeat?

B. What is the last digit in the decimal for $\frac{2}{3}$ shown on your calculator?

C. Complete this number sentence: $\frac{2}{3} \approx$ ?

D. Place your centiwheel on top of the circle. Use your centiwheel and the circle divided into thirds to find a decimal for $\frac{2}{3}$ (to the nearest hundredth).

290 SG • Grade 5 • Unit 9 • Lesson 1 Fractions and Division

***Student Guide* - page 290**

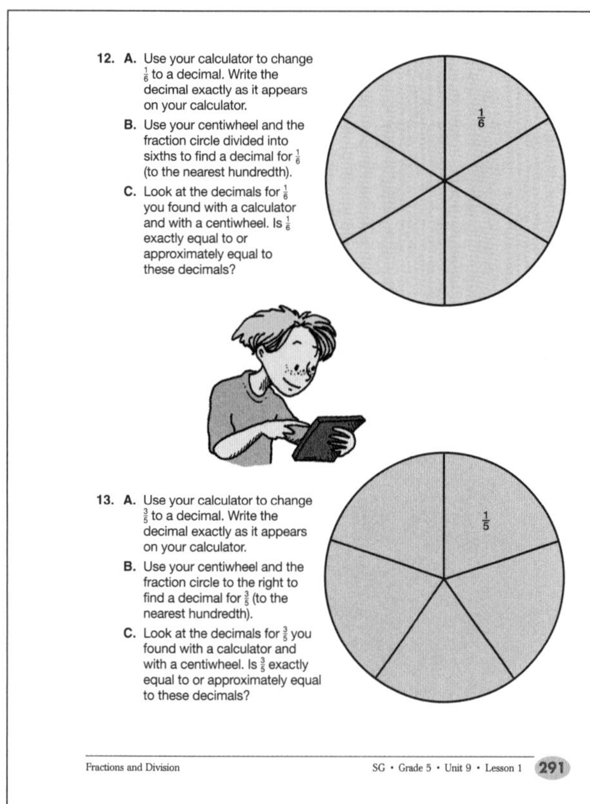

12. A. Use your calculator to change $\frac{1}{6}$ to a decimal. Write the decimal exactly as it appears on your calculator.

B. Use your centiwheel and the fraction circle divided into sixths to find a decimal for $\frac{1}{6}$ (to the nearest hundredth).

C. Look at the decimals for $\frac{1}{6}$ you found with a calculator and with a centiwheel. Is $\frac{1}{6}$ exactly equal to or approximately equal to these decimals?

13. A. Use your calculator to change $\frac{3}{5}$ to a decimal. Write the decimal exactly as it appears on your calculator.

B. Use your centiwheel and the fraction circle to the right to find a decimal for $\frac{3}{5}$ (to the nearest hundredth).

C. Look at the decimals for $\frac{3}{5}$ you found with a calculator and with a centiwheel. Is $\frac{3}{5}$ exactly equal to or approximately equal to these decimals?

Fractions and Division SG • Grade 5 • Unit 9 • Lesson 1 291

***Student Guide* - page 291**

*Answers and/or discussion are included in the Lesson Guide.

## Student Guide (p. 290)

10. A. It has a repeating digit, 3.

B. No; $\frac{1}{3} \approx 0.3333333$

C. 0.33; See Figure 6 in Lesson Guide 1.*

11. A. 6

B. Many calculators will show a 7.

C. $\frac{2}{3} \approx 0.6666667$

D.

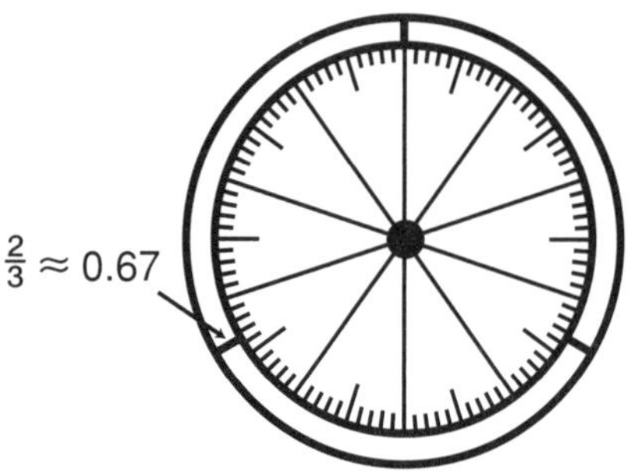


## Student Guide (p. 291)

12. A. 0.1666667 (Many calculators will show 0.1666667.)

B.

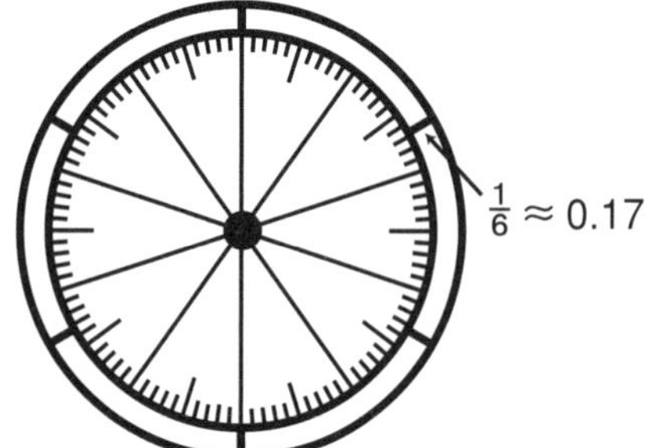


C. Approximately equal. The decimal has a repeating digit, 6.

13. A. 0.6

B.

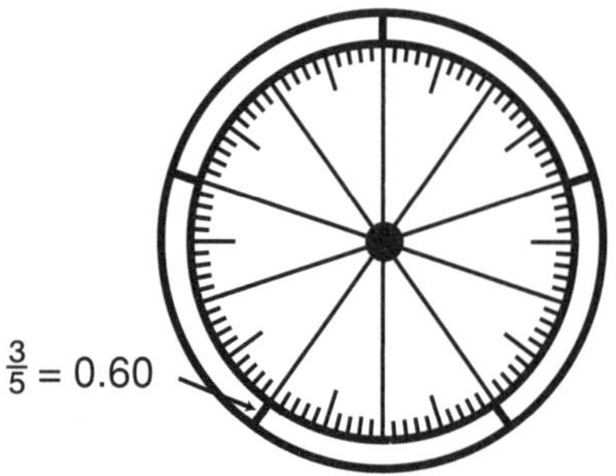


C. Equal. There is no repeating digit, and the decimal terminates after 6.

## Student Guide (p. 292)

**14. A.** 0.375

**B.**

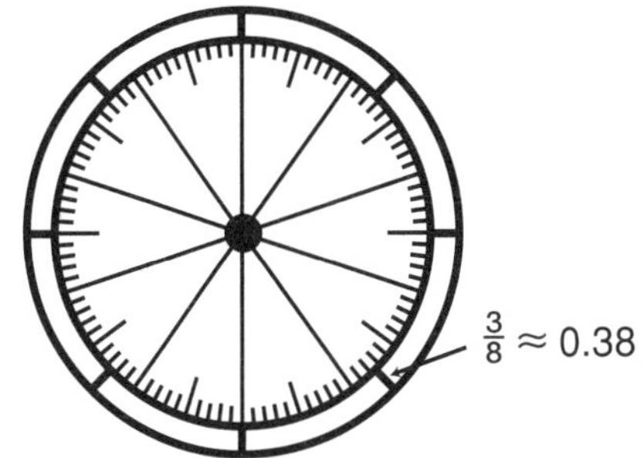


**C.** Equal. The decimal terminates after 5 and there is no repeating digit.

**D.** Approximately equal; 0.375 is rounded to the nearest hundredth to get 0.38.

**15. A.** 0.625

**B.** 0.625

**C.** Yes. The decimal equivalent of each fraction is the same.

**D.** No. The decimal equivalent of each fraction is not the same.

**E.** Find the decimal equivalent of each fraction. If both decimals are equivalent, the fractions are equivalent.

**16.** $\frac{15}{20}, \frac{75}{100}, \frac{12}{16}$

**17.** $\frac{6}{9}, \frac{44}{66}$*

**18. A.** $\frac{140}{160}$ and **C.** $\frac{875}{1000}$

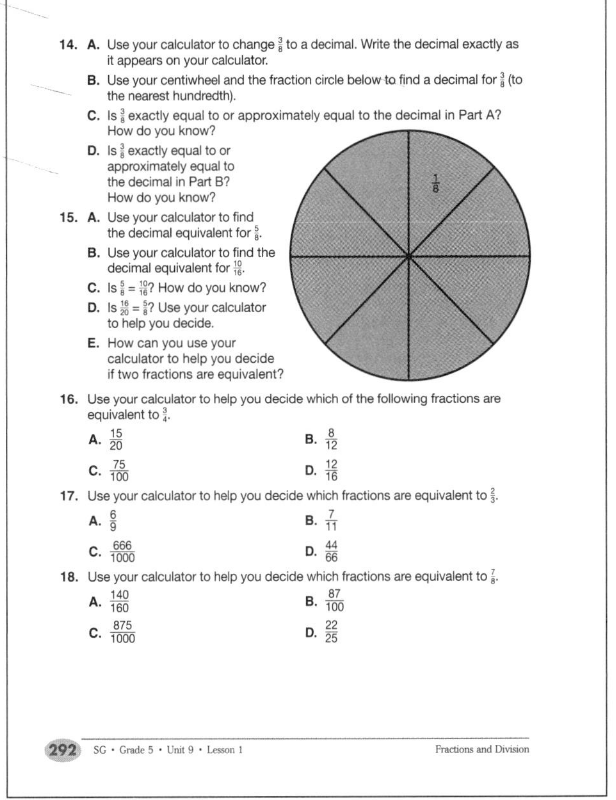

**14. A.** Use your calculator to change $\frac{3}{8}$ to a decimal. Write the decimal exactly as it appears on your calculator.

**B.** Use your centiwheel and the fraction circle below to find a decimal for $\frac{3}{8}$ (to the nearest hundredth).

**C.** Is $\frac{3}{8}$ exactly equal to or approximately equal to the decimal in Part A? How do you know?

**D.** Is $\frac{3}{8}$ exactly equal to or approximately equal to the decimal in Part B? How do you know?

**15. A.** Use your calculator to find the decimal equivalent for $\frac{5}{8}$.

**B.** Use your calculator to find the decimal equivalent for $\frac{10}{16}$.

**C.** Is $\frac{5}{8} = \frac{10}{16}$? How do you know?

**D.** Is $\frac{16}{20} = \frac{5}{8}$? Use your calculator to help you decide.

**E.** How can you use your calculator to help you decide if two fractions are equivalent?



**16.** Use your calculator to help you decide which of the following fractions are equivalent to $\frac{3}{4}$.

**A.** $\frac{15}{20}$ **B.** $\frac{8}{12}$

**C.** $\frac{75}{100}$ **D.** $\frac{12}{16}$

**17.** Use your calculator to help you decide which fractions are equivalent to $\frac{2}{3}$.

**A.** $\frac{6}{9}$ **B.** $\frac{7}{11}$

**C.** $\frac{666}{1000}$ **D.** $\frac{44}{66}$

**18.** Use your calculator to help you decide which fractions are equivalent to $\frac{7}{8}$.

**A.** $\frac{140}{160}$ **B.** $\frac{87}{100}$

**C.** $\frac{875}{1000}$ **D.** $\frac{22}{25}$

292 SG • Grade 5 • Unit 9 • Lesson 1 Fractions and Division

***Student Guide* - page 292**

*Answers and/or discussion are included in the Lesson Guide.

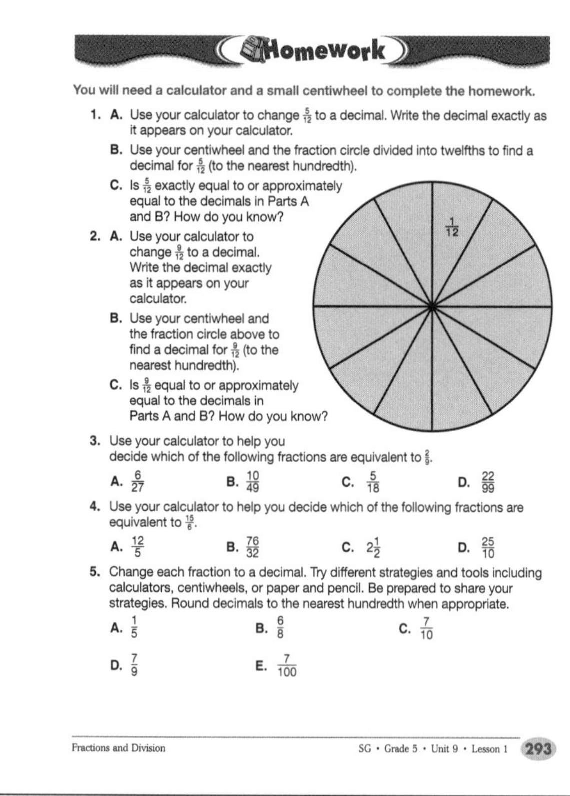

Homework

You will need a calculator and a small centiwheel to complete the homework.

1. A. Use your calculator to change $\frac{5}{12}$ to a decimal. Write the decimal exactly as it appears on your calculator.
   B. Use your centiwheel and the fraction circle divided into twelfths to find a decimal for $\frac{5}{12}$ (to the nearest hundredth).
   C. Is $\frac{5}{12}$ exactly equal to or approximately equal to the decimals in Parts A and B? How do you know?
2. A. Use your calculator to change $\frac{9}{12}$ to a decimal. Write the decimal exactly as it appears on your calculator.
   B. Use your centiwheel and the fraction circle above to find a decimal for $\frac{9}{12}$ (to the nearest hundredth).
   C. Is $\frac{9}{12}$ equal to or approximately equal to the decimals in Parts A and B? How do you know?
3. Use your calculator to help you decide which of the following fractions are equivalent to $\frac{2}{9}$.
   A. $\frac{6}{27}$ B. $\frac{10}{49}$ C. $\frac{5}{18}$ D. $\frac{22}{99}$
4. Use your calculator to help you decide which of the following fractions are equivalent to $\frac{15}{6}$.
   A. $\frac{12}{5}$ B. $\frac{76}{32}$ C. $2\frac{1}{2}$ D. $\frac{25}{10}$
5. Change each fraction to a decimal. Try different strategies and tools including calculators, centiwheels, or paper and pencil. Be prepared to share your strategies. Round decimals to the nearest hundredth when appropriate.
   A. $\frac{1}{5}$ B. $\frac{6}{8}$ C. $\frac{7}{10}$
   D. $\frac{7}{9}$ E. $\frac{7}{100}$

Fractions and Division SG • Grade 5 • Unit 9 • Lesson 1 293

*Student Guide* - page 293

## Student Guide (p. 293)

### Homework

1. A. Many calculators will show 0.4166667.
   B.

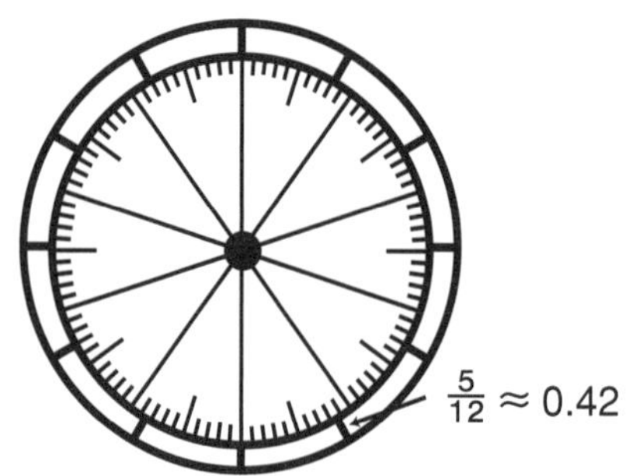


   C. Approximately equal. There is a repeating digit, 6.
2. A. 0.75
   B.

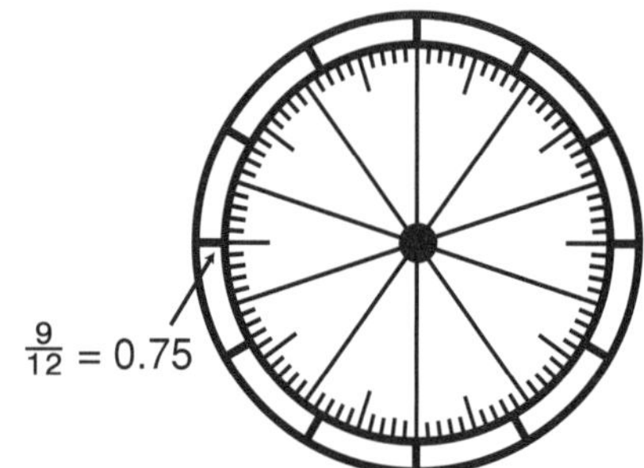


   C. Equal. The decimal terminates after 5 and there is no repeating digit.
3. $\frac{6}{27}$, $\frac{22}{99}$
4. $2\frac{1}{2}$, $\frac{25}{10}$
5. A. 0.2
   B. 0.75
   C. 0.7
   D. 0.78
   E. 0.07

## Discovery Assignment Book (p. 147)

### Home Practice*

### Part 1. Division Practice

A. 720 R2 Possible strategy: $5762 \div 8 \approx 5600 \div 8$ or 700

B. 140 R3

C. 1563 R2

D. 1063

Name ______ Date ______

**Unit 9** Home Practice

**PART 1** Division Practice

**Solve each problem using paper and pencil. Estimate to see if your answers are reasonable. Explain your estimation strategy for Question A.**

A. $5762 \div 8 =$ B. $1263 \div 9 =$

C. $4691 \div 3 =$ D. $3189 \div 3 =$

**PART 2** Fractions and Decimals

1. Find a pair of equivalent fractions in each set. You may use a calculator or another strategy. Be prepared to explain your thinking.

A. $\frac{7}{15}$ $\frac{28}{75}$ $\frac{79}{160}$ $\frac{21}{45}$

B. $\frac{15}{20}$ $\frac{125}{200}$ $\frac{3}{5}$ $\frac{27}{45}$

C. $\frac{1}{3}$ $\frac{33}{100}$ $\frac{4}{5}$ $\frac{11}{33}$

D. $\frac{6}{16}$ $\frac{24}{36}$ $\frac{36}{112}$ $\frac{66}{176}$

2. Use your calculator to change each fraction to a decimal (to the nearest hundredth). Then change each decimal to a percent.

| | Decimal | Percent |
|---|---|---|
| A. $\frac{4}{5}$ | ______ | ______ |
| B. $\frac{7}{12}$ | ______ | ______ |
| C. $\frac{4}{15}$ | ______ | ______ |



CONNECTIONS TO DIVISION DAB • Grade 5 • Unit 9 **147**

*Discovery Assignment Book* - page 147

## Discovery Assignment Book (p. 151)

### Dividing Pizzas

1. A. $\frac{1}{4}$

   B. $1 \div 4 = \frac{1}{4}$

2. A. $\frac{3}{4}$

   B. $3 \div 4 = \frac{3}{4}$

Name ______ Date ______

**Dividing Pizzas**

1. Lin is planning a sleep-over. Her mother says she can invite 3 girls to spend the night so there will be 4 girls in all. Lin wants to order pizzas, but is not sure how many to order. Answer the following questions. Draw a picture when it helps.

   A. If Lin orders one pizza and the girls split it evenly, what fraction of the pizza will each of the girls get?

   B. Write the division number sentence that this fraction represents. Use the boxes as a guide.

   $\square \div \square = \frac{\square}{\square}$

2. A. If Lin orders three pizzas and the girls split them fairly, what fraction of one pizza will each girl get?

   B. Write the division number sentence that this fraction represents. Use the boxes as a guide.

   $\square \div \square = \frac{\square}{\square}$



Fractions and Division DAB • Grade 5 • Unit 9 • Lesson 1 **151**

*Discovery Assignment Book* - page 151

*Answers for all the Home Practice in the *Discovery Assignment Book* are at the end of the unit.

Name ______________________ Date ______________

3. The table below shows what happens when you share four pizzas with more and more people. Complete each column. Draw pictures when it helps.

Sharing Pizzas

| Number of Pizzas | Number of People | Number of Pizzas Each Person Will Get | Division Number Sentence |
|---|---|---|---|
| 4 | 1 | | |
| 4 | 2 | | $4 \div 2 = 2$ |
| 4 | 3 | | |
| 4 | 4 | $\frac{4 \text{ pizzas}}{4 \text{ people}} =$ 1 pizza per person | |
| 4 | 5 | | |
| 4 | 10 | | |
| 4 | 20 | | |

4. Look at the chart. Describe the patterns you see.



152 DAB • Grade 5 • Unit 9 • Lesson 1 Fractions and Division

*Discovery Assignment Book* - page 152

## Discovery Assignment Book (p. 152)

3. Sharing Pizzas

| Number of Pizzas | Number of People | Number of Pizzas Each Person Will Get | Division Number Sentence |
|---|---|---|---|
| 4 | 1 | $\frac{4 \text{ pizzas}}{1 \text{ person}} =$ 4 pizzas per person | $4 \div 1 = 4$ |
| 4 | 2 | $\frac{4 \text{ pizzas}}{2 \text{ people}} =$ 2 pizzas per person | $4 \div 2 = 2$ |
| 4 | 3 | $\frac{4 \text{ pizzas}}{3 \text{ people}} =$ $\frac{4}{3} = 1\frac{1}{3}$ pizzas per person | $4 \div 3 = \frac{4}{3} = 1\frac{1}{3}$ |
| 4 | 4 | $\frac{4 \text{ pizzas}}{4 \text{ people}} =$ 1 pizza per person | $4 \div 4 = 1$ |
| 4 | 5 | $\frac{4 \text{ pizzas}}{5 \text{ people}} =$ $\frac{4}{5}$ pizzas per person | $4 \div 5 = \frac{4}{5}$ |
| 4 | 10 | $\frac{4 \text{ pizzas}}{10 \text{ people}} =$ $\frac{4}{10}$ pizzas per person | $4 \div 10 = \frac{4}{10}$ |
| 4 | 20 | $\frac{4 \text{ pizzas}}{20 \text{ people}} =$ $\frac{4}{20}$ pizzas per person | $4 \div 20 = \frac{4}{20}$ |

4. As the number of people increases, the amount of pizza per person becomes smaller.

# Division

## Lesson Overview

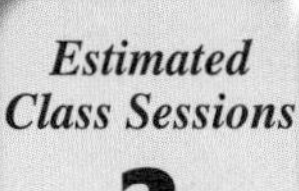

Estimated Class Sessions

**3**

Students review the forgiving method for division. They solve division problems with two-digit divisors using this paper-and-pencil method. Estimation strategies for choosing partial quotients are emphasized.

## Key Content

- Dividing with 2-digit divisors using paper and pencil.
- Checking division using *Quotient* × *Divisor* + *Remainder* = *Dividend.*
- Using estimation to choose more accurate numbers in the partial quotients.
- Estimating quotients.

## Key Vocabulary

- dividend
- divisor
- quotient
- remainder

## Math Facts

DPP item G provides practice with the division facts for the 5s and 10s.

## Homework

1. Assign the *More Estimation and Division* Activity Page in the *Discovery Assignment Book.*
2. Assign the Homework section in the *Student Guide.*
3. Assign Part 2 of the Home Practice.
4. Assign DPP Task J.

## Assessment

1. Use the Homework section of the *Student Guide* as an assessment.
2. Note students' abilities to estimate quotients and to divide using a paper-and-pencil method.

# Curriculum Sequence

## Before This Unit

Students reviewed the forgiving method with one-digit divisors in Unit 4 Lesson 3. Interpreting remainders was also discussed.

## After This Unit

Division practice will be included in the Daily Practice and Problems and Home Practice in all succeeding units.

# Materials List

## Supplies and Copies

| Student | Teacher |
|---|---|
| **Supplies for Each Student**<br>• base-ten pieces, optional | **Supplies** |
| **Copies** | **Copies/Transparencies**<br>• 1 transparency of *Introducing Division,* optional (*Unit Resource Guide* Page 58) |

*All blackline masters including assessment, transparency, and DPP masters are also on the Teacher Resource CD.*

## Student Books

*Division* (*Student Guide* Pages 294–298)
*Estimation and Division* (*Discovery Assignment Book* Page 153)
*More Estimation and Division* (*Discovery Assignment Book* Page 155)

## Daily Practice and Problems and Home Practice

DPP items E–J (*Unit Resource Guide* Pages 16–19)
Home Practice Part 2 (*Discovery Assignment Book* Page 147)

Note: Classrooms whose pacing differs significantly from the suggested pacing of the units should use the Math Facts Calendar in Section 4 of the *Facts Resource Guide* to ensure students receive the complete math facts program.

## Assessment Tools

*Observational Assessment Record* (*Unit Resource Guide* Pages 11–12)

# Daily Practice and Problems

Suggestions for using the DPPs are on page 55.

## E. Bit: Estimating with Ease (URG p. 16)

See if you can figure out these problems in your head. Then write down your reasoning for each answer.

1. About how many 12s are in 140?
2. About how many 25s are in 370?
3. About how many 20s are in 345?

## F. Challenge: Tenths, Hundredths, and Thousandths (URG p. 17)

1. Name a decimal that is greater than 0.3 but less than 0.35.
2. Name a decimal that is greater than 0.25 but less than 0.26.
3. Name a decimal that is greater than 0.403 but less than 0.41.
4. Name a fraction that is greater than $\frac{57}{100}$ but less than $\frac{7}{10}$.
5. Name a fraction that is greater than $\frac{8}{16}$ but less than 0.8.
6. Name a fraction that is greater than 17% but less than 0.2.

## G. Bit: Practicing the Facts (URG p. 17)

A. $300 \div 50 =$ B. $400 \div 4 =$

C. $150 \div 3 =$ D. $100 \div 10 =$

E. $45 \div 5 =$ F. $2500 \div 5 =$

G. $600 \div 100 =$ H. $35 \div 7 =$

I. $10 \div 5 =$

## H. Challenge: Craft Fair (URG p. 18)

1. Lee Yah and Manny are setting up tables for the fifth-grade family craft show. Each table is 200 cm long. Tables will line up along two sides of the room. Both sides of the room are 12 meters long. Each participant who wishes to sell crafts pays a $15 rental fee for one table or $25 for two tables. Mr. Moreno tells the students that all the tables are rented. Only 2 people rented two tables. How much money will the school make on the craft show?
2. The community craft show will be held in the gym next month. The school is charging $25 for one table and will have five times as many tables as the fifth-grade craft show. How much will the school make for hosting the community craft show if all of the tables are rented?

## I. Bit: Fractions, Decimals, and the Calculator (URG p. 18)

Use a calculator to change each of the following fractions to decimals. Then compare the decimals to see if each pair of fractions are equivalent.

A. $\frac{4}{7}$ and $\frac{3}{5}$ B. $\frac{1}{3}$ and $\frac{13}{39}$

C. $\frac{12}{15}$ and $\frac{8}{11}$

## J. Task: Division Practice (URG p. 19)

Use estimation to help you divide. Use a paper-and-pencil method or mental math. Show how you check your work.

A. $23 \overline{)756}$ B. $20 \overline{)4000}$

C. $42 \overline{)8973}$ D. $75 \overline{)684}$

## TIMS Tip

If students learned and are proficient with a different paper-and-pencil division method, allow them to use it to solve problems. However, we recommend that they still work through the questions with the forgiving method. Answering questions about the forgiving method will improve their understanding of the division process.

## Content Note

**Vocabulary Review.** In the division problem $8\overline{)96}$, 8 is the **divisor** (the number you are dividing by) and 96 is the **dividend** (the number to be divided). The answer to a division problem is called the **quotient.**

## TIMS Tip

Remind students of how they solved division problems with the base-ten pieces in Unit 4. In this problem you would need to distribute 9 skinnies and 6 bits into 8 groups (the rows). If needed, demonstrate the problem with the base-ten pieces or have students complete the problem with the base-ten pieces.

## Before the Activity

Use DPP item E to start the lesson on the first day. This item gives students practice using multiples of ten to estimate quotients.

## Teaching the Activity

### Part 1 Introducing Division

Use the problems on the *Introducing Division* transparency to begin this lesson. When you display the transparency, cover all but the statement of the first problem. This problem is a review of the forgiving method. Ask:

- *What does each number in this problem stand for?* (96 is the number of students attending the play; 8 is the number of seats in each row or the number of students that can sit in each row.)
- *Copy the problem* $8\overline{)96}$ *onto a piece of paper and find the answer using the forgiving method. Explain your strategies for choosing the partial quotients.* (Possible responses: guessing, using multiplication facts, e.g., $8 \times 5 = 40$, $8 \times 9 = 72$, $8 \times 11 = 88$, or using multiples of 10, $8 \times 10 = 80$.)

Discuss the efficiency of the strategies they choose. Point out that choosing partial quotients that bring us closer to the final quotient and choosing numbers that lend themselves to mental computation are often more efficient. Complete the problem on the transparency using one or more of the suggested strategies as shown in Figure 7.

```
     12              12              12
 8 | 96   |      8 | 96   |      8 | 96   |
   – 40   |  5     – 88   | 11     – 80   | 10
     56   |           8   |          16   |
   – 40   |  5      – 8   |  1     – 16   |  2
     16   |           0     12        0     12
   – 16   |  2
      0     12
```

**Figure 7:** *Three possible paths for solving 96 ÷ 8*

Ask:

- *What information does the quotient give us in this problem?* (12 rows are needed and they will be completely filled.)
- *How can you check your work?* (Since multiplication and division are related, you can check division by multiplying the quotient by the divisor and adding the remainder.)

Emphasize that **(quotient × divisor) + remainder = dividend.** Ask a student to check the division for the first problem on the transparency: $8 \times 12 = 96$. In this problem the remainder is 0 (or we can say no remainder).

Use the second problem on the transparency to introduce two-digit divisors. Stress estimations. Begin by asking:

- *Will the quotient have one, two, or three digits in it?* (Since $10 \times 24 = 240$ and $100 \times 24 = 2400$, guide students to see that the quotient will have two digits because 852 is between 240 and 2400.)

Once students understand that the quotient is between 10 and 99, ask:

- *Estimate a reasonable partial quotient.*

If students are having difficulty with this, suggest using multiples of 10 as one strategy. Using this strategy, 10, 20, or 30 would be reasonable partial quotients to start with. If a student estimates 40 as a partial quotient, show them that this estimate would be too large since $40 \times 24 = 960$.

Other strategies for finding a partial quotient are possible. For example, a student may suggest there are at least thirty-two 24s in 852 since they know that 24 is almost 25 and there are four 25s in every 100. Encourage students to look at many different estimation strategies and to choose one they are comfortable with and is the most efficient to use.

Start the problem using a partial quotient suggested by a student. One possible starting point is shown in Figure 8. Remind them that the 480 means that 480 apples are taken care of (boxed) and 372 remain to be boxed.

```
24 | 852  |
   - 480  | 20
     372
```

**Figure 8:** *One possible partial quotient*

Ask students to estimate how many more boxes you need for the remaining apples. Depending on the first partial quotient used, students might use multiples of 10 again, or they may need to use a number smaller than 10. Continue finding partial quotients until the problem is complete. Once students find all the partial quotients, they should add them together to find the solution to the problem (the quotient). Three possible solution paths are shown in Figure 9.

|  | 35 R12 |  |
|---|---|---|
| 24 | 852 |  |
|  | − 480 | 20 |
|  | 372 |  |
|  | − 240 | 10 |
|  | 132 |  |
|  | − 120 | 5 |
|  | 12 | 35 |

|  | 35 R12 |  |
|---|---|---|
| 24 | 852 |  |
|  | − 720 | 30 |
|  | 132 |  |
|  | − 120 | 5 |
|  | 12 | 35 |

|  | 35 R12 |  |
|---|---|---|
| 24 | 852 |  |
|  | − 240 | 10 |
|  | 612 |  |
|  | − 240 | 10 |
|  | 372 |  |
|  | − 240 | 10 |
|  | 132 |  |
|  | − 120 | 5 |
|  | 12 | 35 |

**Figure 9:** *Three possible paths for solving 852 ÷ 24*

Discuss:

- *Use multiplication to check the division.* (See Figure 10.)
- *What does the quotient mean?* (There are 35 complete boxes of apples with 12 apples remaining.)

| 35 | 840 |
|---|---|
| × 24 | + 12 |
| 20 | 852 |
| 120 |  |
| 100 |  |
| 600 |  |
| 840 |  |

**Figure 10:** *Using multiplication to check a division problem*

After completing the transparency, students begin the *Division* Activity Pages in the *Student Guide.* In this lesson, students continue working with two-digit divisors. Read the short vignette together. Have students answer the questions in pairs before discussing them as a class.

## Division

**Planning Ahead**

The fifth-grade classes at Bessie Coleman Elementary School are planning a dinner for their parents. Brandon, Arti, and Manny are on the food committee. They are meeting with Mr. Cline, one of the school's cooks. He is helping them plan a menu that includes an enchilada casserole, a salad, and a dessert.

"Each casserole pan will serve an average of 32 people," said Mr. Cline. "If you know how many people you expect to serve, you can figure out how many pans of the enchilada casserole you will need to prepare."

"Three hundred eighty-nine people said that they will come," said Arti.

294 SG • Grade 5 • Unit 9 • Lesson 2 Division

***Student Guide* - page 294**

In ***Question 1,*** students use multiples of 10 to estimate the number of pans of casserole they will need. If 10 pans are prepared, students will be able to serve 320 people, and if 20 pans are prepared they will be able to serve 640 people. Since they are only expecting 389 people, 10 is a better estimate—preparing 20 pans would be too much food. Discuss how Brandon records his work using the forgiving method ***(Questions 1E–1F).*** The 320 tells the number of people that 10 pans of enchilada casserole will serve; 69 shows the number of people who still need to be taken care of.

In ***Question 2,*** Arti estimates that they will need to make at least two more pans of enchilada casserole. Discuss her recorded work.

Discuss:

- *Why does Manny think they should make 13 pans of enchilada casserole instead of 12 pans?* (If 2 more pans were made, 64 more people could be served but 5 still do not get any casserole. The 5 is the **remainder.**)

***Question 3*** leads students through a second division problem. For ***Questions 3A–3B,*** students tell what the numbers in this problem represent. The number 24 can be either the pounds of clay or the number of students for each block of clay. The number 531 is the number of art students in the school.

Mrs. Sorenson uses multiples of 25 to estimate her answer. In ***Question 3C,*** Mrs. Sorenson starts to find an exact answer. She records her work showing that 20 blocks will provide clay for 480 students; however, 51 students will not get clay unless she orders more blocks. In ***Question 3D,*** Mrs. Sorenson estimates she will need at least 2 more blocks of clay. Since her work shows that 3 students still remain without clay, Mrs. Sorenson needs to order 23 blocks of clay ***(Question 3F).***

## Part 2 Dividing with Larger Dividends

Once you complete ***Questions 1–3*** in the *Student Guide,* ask:

- *What numbers might you use to estimate the quotient in the problem 8656 ÷ 42?* (Students should suggest using multiples of 100 to estimate.)
- *What multiple of 100 would be a good estimate to start with?*

"This sounds like a division problem," said Manny. "To figure out the number of pans we need to prepare, we need to divide the total number of people we expect by the number of servings each pan will make."

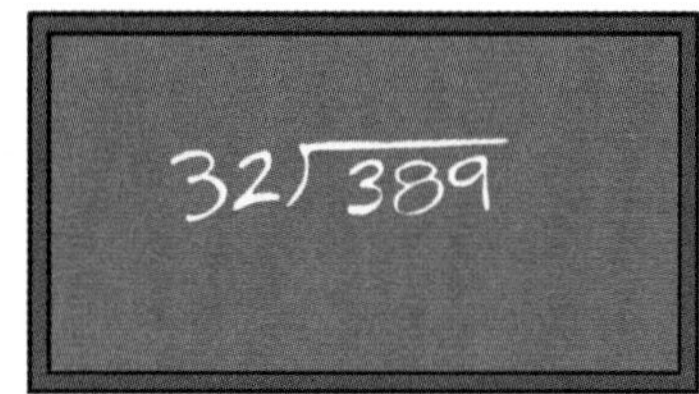

"I know how to do this," Brandon exclaimed. "First we need to decide how many groups of 32 there are in 389. I think a good way to do this is to estimate with multiples of 10."

1. A. If Mr. Cline prepares 10 pans of enchilada casserole, how many people can the fifth grade serve?
   B. Are 10 pans too much or too little?
   C. How many people can they serve if Mr. Cline prepares 20 pans of enchilada casserole?
   D. Are 20 pans too much or too little?

Brandon decided to start the division problem by estimating that they would need at least 10 pans of enchilada casserole. He recorded his work.

```
32⟌389  |
  -320  | 10
    69
```

   E. If Mr. Cline made only 10 pans of casserole, how many people would not get served?
   F. How did Brandon record this?

Division SG • Grade 5 • Unit 9 • Lesson 2 295

**Student Guide - page 295** ***(Answers on p. 59)***

"I think that we will need to make at least two more pans of enchilada casserole in order to feed everyone," said Arti. Arti recorded her work.

```
      12 R5
32⟌389  |
  -320  | 10
    69  |
   -64  |  2
     5    12
```

2. A. If Mr. Cline makes two more pans of casserole, how many more people can be served?
   B. How many people will not be served?

"This shows that we need to make 10 + 2 or 12 pans of enchilada casserole to serve 320 + 64 or 384 people," said Manny. "We still have 5 people who will be without food. 5 is the remainder. Since we don't want anyone to be without food, Mr. Cline needs to make 1 more pan of casserole, or a total of 13 pans."

Arti remembered that she could check her division by multiplying the **quotient** by the **divisor** and adding the **remainder:** 12 × 32 + 5 = 389. Arti's computation gave her the **dividend** 389, so she knew her division was correct.

### Ordering Clay

The art teacher at Ontario School, Mrs. Sorenson, is ordering clay for the school.

Clay comes in 24-pound blocks. She knows that each student uses an average of 1 pound of clay each year. This year there are 531 art students. Mrs. Sorenson knows that she needs to divide 531 by 24 to find out how many blocks of clay she needs to order.

3. A. What does the number 24 tell us in this problem?
   B. What does the number 531 tell us in this problem?

296 SG • Grade 5 • Unit 9 • Lesson 2 Division

**Student Guide - page 296** ***(Answers on p. 59)***

Mrs. Sorenson knows that 24 is close to 25 and that there are four 25s in 100. So she decides to use multiples of 25 to estimate how many blocks of clay she should order. Mrs. Sorenson estimates that she should order at least 20 blocks of clay, since there are twenty 25s in 500.

**C.** If she orders only 20 blocks of clay, how many students will not get clay this year?

```
24 | 531 |
   - 480 | 20
      51
```

**D.** Mrs. Sorenson sees that she needs to order at least two more blocks of clay. She records her second estimate. Is this enough clay to make sure that each student will get clay? Explain your answer.

```
      22 R3
24 | 531 |
   - 480 | 20
      51 |
   -  48 |  2
       3   22
```

**E.** Write a number sentence to check the division.

**F.** How much clay should Mrs. Sorenson order so that every child will get clay? Explain your answer.

**Complete the following problems. Use estimation to help you divide. Record your work using a paper-and-pencil method. Write a number sentence to check your work.**

**4.** The students at Bessie Coleman School are setting up tables for their parent dinner. Students can use either the rectangular tables or the round tables.
- **A.** Each of the rectangular tables will seat 12 people. How many rectangular tables will they need to seat all 389 people?
- **B.** Each of the round tables will seat 10 people. How many round tables will they need to seat all 389 people?

**5.** Alexis, Edward, and Irma are making centerpieces for each table. Each centerpiece will use 24 inches of ribbon. They have a spool with 864 inches of ribbon.
- **A.** How many centerpieces can they make?
- **B.** Will they have enough centerpieces to place one on each of the rectangular tables if they use only rectangular tables? Explain your answer.
- **C.** Will they have enough centerpieces to place one on each of the round tables if they use only round tables? Explain your answer.

Division SG • Grade 5 • Unit 9 • Lesson 2 **297**

***Student Guide* - page 297** *(Answers on p. 60)*

Name ______________________ Date ______________

## Estimation and Division

**Estimate each quotient. Tell what strategy you used to make your estimate.**

Example: 22 ⟌834

Think:

| | |
|---|---|
| 22 × 10 = | 220 |
| 22 × 20 = | 440 |
| 22 × 30 = | 660 |
| 22 × 40 = | 880 |

←834

Answer: I used multiples of 10. Since 834 is between 22 × 30 = 660 and 22 × 40 = 880, the quotient will be at least 30 but less than 40.

**1.** 11 ⟌258 **2.** 21 ⟌753

**3.** 32 ⟌568 **4.** 25 ⟌648

**5.** 42 ⟌3253 **6.** 38 ⟌6206

**7.** 50 ⟌792 **8.** 73 ⟌7890



Division DAB • Grade 5 • Unit 9 • Lesson 2 **153**

***Discovery Assignment Book* - page 153** *(Answers on p. 62)*

Have students check their estimates using mental math as they did in ***Question 1.*** Students might think: 42 × 100 = 4200; 42 × 200 = 8400; 42 × 300 = 12,600. Good estimates are either 100 or 200. The most efficient estimate is 200. Record this and then complete the problem by using further estimations. One possible solution is shown in Figure 11.

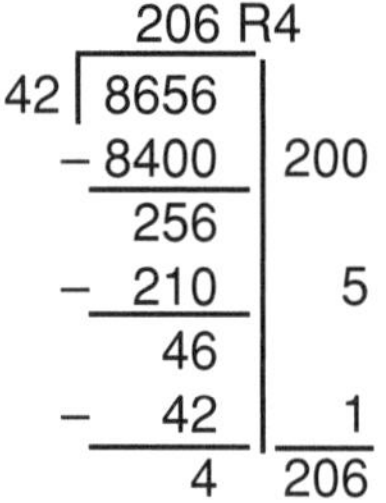


**Figure 11:** *One path for completing this division problem using the forgiving method*

### Part 3 Practicing Estimation

To give students more practice using estimation to begin division, assign the *Estimation and Division* Activity Page in the *Discovery Assignment Book.* Solve a problem from this page with the class before asking students to complete the remaining problems independently or in groups. Emphasize that students need only find an estimate. Good estimates will make efficient partial products when they begin a division problem.

Assign the *More Estimation and Division* page for homework. Remind students to find efficient estimates and to explain their strategies.

### Part 4 Practicing Division

Students can work on ***Questions 4–7*** in the Explore section of the *Student Guide* independently or with a partner. One often successful strategy is to have students complete the work independently and then compare work with a partner. Both partners should be able to explain and justify the steps they took to reach their answers.

Remind students to interpret the remainders carefully. For example, ***Question 4A*** asks how many tables are needed to seat 389 people if 12 people can sit at one table. Since 389 ÷ 12 = 32 R5, 33 tables are needed to seat all 389 people.

Students should choose efficient strategies to solve each problem. For example, for ***Question 7D*** students can reason that there are two 50s in one hundred and eighteen 50s in 900.

Homework ***Questions 1–11*** provide practice using a paper-and-pencil method for division. Encourage students to use estimation as they work through each step of these problems. They will check their work in ***Questions 1–6*** using multiplication. ***Questions 7–11*** provide an opportunity for students to use division to solve problems. They need to think about the remainders in these problems to answer the questions.

### Journal Prompt

If you were planning a party and needed to purchase party favors, plates, cups, and napkins, how could division help you find out how much you need to buy? Give examples to help explain your thoughts.

## Math Facts

DPP item G provides practice with the division facts for the 5s and 10s.

## Homework and Practice

- DPP Bit E provides practice estimating quotients.
- The *More Estimation and Division* Activity Page in the *Discovery Assignment Book* can be assigned as homework after Part 3 of the lesson.
- Use DPP items F, H, I, and J to review concepts including fractions, decimals, problem solving, and division.
- Assign homework ***Questions 1–11*** in the *Student Guide* after completing Part 4 of the lesson.
- Assign Part 2 of the Home Practice that reviews fractions and decimals.

*Answers for Part 2 of the Home Practice are in the Answer Key at the end of this lesson and at the end of this unit.*

6. The plates that the students will use come in packages of 48.
   A. How many packages will they need to serve all 389 people?
   B. How many plates will be left over?
7. A. 39 ⟌873 B. 12 ⟌3706
   C. 26 ⟌785 D. 50 ⟌900

### Homework

For Questions 1–6:

A. Use a paper-and-pencil method or mental math to solve each division problem. Record all your work on your paper.

B. Check your answer using a different method. Write a number sentence to show how you checked your work.

1. 20 ⟌163 2. 36 ⟌952 3. 40 ⟌8000
4. 56 ⟌598 5. 45 ⟌3607 6. 23 ⟌4594
7. Jackie has chosen a 364-page book from the library. She wants to finish reading it in two weeks. How many pages should she plan to read each day?
8. Mr. Moreno asked Edward and Roberto to help him divide 943 marbles evenly among 15 bags.
   A. How many marbles will be in each bag?
   B. Will there be any marbles left over? If so, how many?
9. Mr. Moreno wanted to know the average number of miles he traveled each day. He kept track of the miles he traveled and found that in a two-week period he traveled 882 miles. What is the average number of miles he traveled each day?
10. Mr. Cline is making rolls for the school lunch. He needs 465 rolls. Each package contains 12 rolls. How many packages should he prepare?
11. Mrs. Sorenson is cutting ribbon for an art project. She has 650 cm of ribbon. Each student needs a strip 15 cm long. How many strips can she cut?

298 SG • Grade 5 • Unit 9 • Lesson 2 Division

***Student Guide* - page 298 *(Answers on p. 61)***

Name ______________________ Date ______________

### More Estimation and Division

**Estimate each quotient. Tell what strategy you used to make your estimate.**

Example: 27 ⟌8432

Think:

| | |
|---|---|
| 25 × 200 = | 5000 |
| 25 × 300 = | 7500 |
| 25 × 400 = | 10,000 |

← 8432

Possible answer: Use 25 as a convenient number for 27. I tried multiples of 100. Since 8432 is between 25 × 300 and 25 × 400, the quotient is between 300 and 400.

1. 12 ⟌497 2. 79 ⟌9898
3. 52 ⟌6449 4. 26 ⟌8970
5. 17 ⟌874 6. 32 ⟌9583



Division DAB • Grade 5 • Unit 9 • Lesson 2 155

***Discovery Assignment Book* - page 155 *(Answers on p. 63)***

Name ______________________ Date ______________

# Unit 9 Home Practice

**PART 1 Division Practice**

**Solve each problem using paper and pencil. Estimate to see if your answers are reasonable. Explain your estimation strategy for Question A.**

A. $5762 \div 8 =$ B. $1263 \div 9 =$

C. $4691 \div 3 =$ D. $3189 \div 3 =$

**PART 2 Fractions and Decimals**

1. Find a pair of equivalent fractions in each set. You may use a calculator or another strategy. Be prepared to explain your thinking.

A. $\frac{7}{15}$ $\frac{28}{75}$ $\frac{79}{160}$ $\frac{21}{45}$

B. $\frac{15}{20}$ $\frac{125}{200}$ $\frac{3}{5}$ $\frac{27}{45}$

C. $\frac{1}{3}$ $\frac{33}{100}$ $\frac{4}{5}$ $\frac{11}{33}$

D. $\frac{6}{16}$ $\frac{24}{36}$ $\frac{36}{112}$ $\frac{66}{176}$

2. Use your calculator to change each fraction to a decimal (to the nearest hundredth). Then change each decimal to a percent.

| | Decimal | Percent |
|---|---|---|
| A. $\frac{4}{5}$ | ________ | ________ |
| B. $\frac{7}{12}$ | ________ | ________ |
| C. $\frac{4}{15}$ | ________ | ________ |





***Discovery Assignment Book* - page 147** *(Answers on p. 62)*

## Assessment

- Use the Homework section in the *Student Guide* to assess students' understanding of a paper-and-pencil method to compute division problems.
- Use the *Observational Assessment Record* to note students' abilities to estimate quotients and to divide using a paper-and-pencil method.

Estimated Class Sessions **3**

# At a Glance

## Math Facts and Daily Practice and Problems

DPP item G provides practice with the division facts for the 5s and 10s. Items E, F, H, I, and J review concepts including area, decimals, problem solving, fractions, and estimation.

## Before the Activity

Use Bit E to begin the lesson. It provides practice with estimating quotients.

## Part 1. Introducing Division

1. Use the problems on the *Introducing Division* transparency in the *Unit Resource Guide* to review the forgiving method for division.
2. Read the vignette on the *Division* Activity Pages in the *Student Guide*. Discuss ***Question 1***. Encourage students to use multiples of 10 as a strategy to estimate the quotient.
3. Discuss the remainder and how it is used in ***Question 2***.
4. Discuss the strategy of using multiples of 25 to estimate. ***(Question 3)***

## Part 2. Dividing with Larger Dividends

Complete the problem 8656 ÷ 42 using multiples of 100 to estimate the quotient.

## Part 3. Practicing Estimation

Assign the *Estimation and Division* Activity Page in the *Discovery Assignment Book*.

## Part 4. Practicing Division

Students answer ***Questions 4–7*** on the *Division* Activity Pages in the *Student Guide*.

## Homework

1. Assign the *More Estimation and Division* Activity Page in the *Discovery Assignment Book*.
2. Assign the Homework section in the *Student Guide*.
3. Assign Part 2 of the Home Practice.
4. Assign DPP Task J.

## Assessment

1. The Homework section of the *Student Guide* can be used as an assessment.
2. Use the *Observational Assessment Record* to note students' abilities to estimate quotients and to divide using a paper-and-pencil method.

*Answer Key is on pages 59–63.*

Notes:

# Introducing Division

1. Ninety-six students from Bessie Coleman Elementary School are attending a play at a local theater. They will sit in rows of 8 seats. How many rows will they need to seat all the students? Will each row be completely filled?

$$8\overline{)96}$$

2. There are 852 apples that need to be packaged into boxes of 24 apples. How many boxes will you need?

$$24\overline{)852}$$

## Student Guide (p. 295)

1. A. 320*
   B. Too little
   C. 640
   D. Too much
   E. 69
   F. Using the forgiving method. He still has 69 to take care of.

"This sounds like a division problem," said Manny. "To figure out the number of pans we need to prepare, we need to divide the total number of people we expect by the number of servings each pan will make."

"I know how to do this," Brandon exclaimed. "First we need to decide how many groups of 32 there are in 389. I think a good way to do this is to estimate with multiples of 10."

1. A. If Mr. Cline prepares 10 pans of enchilada casserole, how many people can the fifth grade serve?
   B. Are 10 pans too much or too little?
   C. How many people can they serve if Mr. Cline prepares 20 pans of enchilada casserole?
   D. Are 20 pans too much or too little?

Brandon decided to start the division problem by estimating that they would need at least 10 pans of enchilada casserole. He recorded his work.

```
32 | 389
   - 320 | 10
      69
```

   E. If Mr. Cline made only 10 pans of casserole, how many people would not get served?
   F. How did Brandon record this?

Division SG • Grade 5 • Unit 9 • Lesson 2  295

*Student Guide* - page 295

## Student Guide (p. 296)

2. A. 64
   B. 5
3. A. The number 24 can be either the pounds of clay or the number of students for each block of clay.*
   B. The number 531 is the number of art students in the school.*

"I think that we will need to make at least two more pans of enchilada casserole in order to feed everyone," said Arti. Arti recorded her work.

```
      12 R5
32 | 389
   - 320 | 10
      69
   -  64 |  2
       5   12
```

2. A. If Mr. Cline makes two more pans of casserole, how many more people can be served?
   B. How many people will not be served?

"This shows that we need to make 10 + 2 or 12 pans of enchilada casserole to serve 320 + 64 or 384 people," said Manny. "We still have 5 people who will be without food. 5 is the remainder. Since we don't want anyone to be without food, Mr. Cline needs to make 1 more pan of casserole, or a total of 13 pans."

Arti remembered that she could check her division by multiplying the **quotient** by the **divisor** and adding the **remainder:** 12 × 32 + 5 = 389. Arti's computation gave her the **dividend** 389, so she knew her division was correct.

### Ordering Clay

The art teacher at Ontario School, Mrs. Sorenson, is ordering clay for the school.

Clay comes in 24-pound blocks. She knows that each student uses an average of 1 pound of clay each year. This year there are 531 art students. Mrs. Sorenson knows that she needs to divide 531 by 24 to find out how many blocks of clay she needs to order.

24⟌531

3. A. What does the number 24 tell us in this problem?
   B. What does the number 531 tell us in this problem?

296 SG • Grade 5 • Unit 9 • Lesson 2 Division

*Student Guide* - page 296

*Answers and/or discussion are included in the Lesson Guide.

Mrs. Sorenson knows that 24 is close to 25 and that there are four 25s in 100. So she decides to use multiples of 25 to estimate how many blocks of clay she should order. Mrs. Sorenson estimates that she should order at least 20 blocks of clay, since there are twenty 25s in 500.

C. If she orders only 20 blocks of clay, how many students will not get clay this year?

```
24| 531  |
  - 480  |20
     51
```

D. Mrs. Sorenson sees that she needs to order at least two more blocks of clay. She records her second estimate. Is this enough clay to make sure that each student will get clay? Explain your answer.

```
      22 R3
24| 531  |
  - 480  |20
     51  |
  -  48  | 2
      3   22
```

E. Write a number sentence to check the division.

F. How much clay should Mrs. Sorenson order so that every child will get clay? Explain your answer.

**Complete the following problems. Use estimation to help you divide. Record your work using a paper-and-pencil method. Write a number sentence to check your work.**

4. The students at Bessie Coleman School are setting up tables for their parent dinner. Students can use either the rectangular tables or the round tables.
   A. Each of the rectangular tables will seat 12 people. How many rectangular tables will they need to seat all 389 people?
   B. Each of the round tables will seat 10 people. How many round tables will they need to seat all 389 people?
5. Alexis, Edward, and Irma are making centerpieces for each table. Each centerpiece will use 24 inches of ribbon. They have a spool with 864 inches of ribbon.
   A. How many centerpieces can they make?
   B. Will they have enough centerpieces to place one on each of the rectangular tables if they use only rectangular tables? Explain your answer.
   C. Will they have enough centerpieces to place one on each of the round tables if they use only round tables? Explain your answer.

Division SG • Grade 5 • Unit 9 • Lesson 2 297

***Student Guide* - page 297**

## Student Guide (p. 297)

3. **C.** 51 students*

   **D.** No. There will still be 3 students who will not get any clay.*

   **E.** $22 \times 24 + 3 = 531$

   **F.** 23 pounds. Since she doesn't want any students without clay, she needs to order one more pound in addition to the 22 pounds.

4. **A.** 33 tables*

```
     32R5
12| 389  |
  - 360  |30
     29  |
  -  24  | 2
      5   32
```

   $32 \times 12 + 5 = 389$

   **B.** 39 tables

```
     38R9
10| 389  |
  - 300  |30
     89  |
  -  80  | 8
      9   38
```

   $38 \times 10 + 9 = 389$

5. **A.** 36

   **B.** Yes. There are only 33 rectangular tables. Each table can have a centerpiece and there will be 3 centerpieces left over.

   **C.** No. There are 39 round tables and only 36 centerpieces.

*Answers and/or discussion are included in the Lesson Guide.

## Student Guide (p. 298)

6. **A.** 9 packages
   **B.** 43 plates
7. **A.** 22 R15; $22 \times 39 + 15 = 873$
   **B.** 308 R10; $308 \times 12 + 10 = 3706$
   **C.** 30 R5; $30 \times 26 + 5 = 785$
   **D.** 18; $18 \times 50 = 900$*

### Homework

For *Questions 1–6*, estimates will vary.

1. $20 \times 8 + 3 = 163$

```
       8R3
 20 | 163 |
    - 100 |  5
       63 |
    -  60 |  3
        3    8
```

2. $26 \times 36 + 16 = 952$

```
       26R16
 36 | 952 |
    - 720 | 20
      232 |
    - 144 |  4
       88 |
       72 |  2
       16   26
```

3. $8000 \div 40 = 200$
   $40 \times 200 = 8000$
4. $10 \times 56 + 38 = 598$

```
       10R38
 56 | 598 |
    - 560 | 10
       38   10
```

5. $80 \times 45 + 7 = 3607$

```
        80R7
 45 | 3607 |
    - 2700 | 60
       907 |
    -  900 | 20
         7   80
```

6. The plates that the students will use come in packages of 48.
   **A.** How many packages will they need to serve all 389 people?
   **B.** How many plates will be left over?
7. **A.** 39 ⟌ 873 **B.** 12 ⟌ 3706
   **C.** 26 ⟌ 785 **D.** 50 ⟌ 900

For Questions 1–6:

**A. Use a paper-and-pencil method or mental math to solve each division problem. Record all your work on your paper.**

**B. Check your answer using a different method. Write a number sentence to show how you checked your work.**

1. 20 ⟌ 163 2. 36 ⟌ 952 3. 40 ⟌ 8000
4. 56 ⟌ 598 5. 45 ⟌ 3607 6. 23 ⟌ 4594

7. Jackie has chosen a 364-page book from the library. She wants to finish reading it in two weeks. How many pages should she plan to read each day?
8. Mr. Moreno asked Edward and Roberto to help him divide 943 marbles evenly among 15 bags.
   **A.** How many marbles will be in each bag?
   **B.** Will there be any marbles left over? If so, how many?
9. Mr. Moreno wanted to know the average number of miles he traveled each day. He kept track of the miles he traveled and found that in a two-week period he traveled 882 miles. What is the average number of miles he traveled each day?
10. Mr. Cline is making rolls for the school lunch. He needs 465 rolls. Each package contains 12 rolls. How many packages should he prepare?
11. Mrs. Sorenson is cutting ribbon for an art project. She has 650 cm of ribbon. Each student needs a strip 15 cm long. How many strips can she cut?

***Student Guide* - page 298**

6. $199 \times 23 + 17 = 4594$

```
        199R17
 23 | 4594 |
    - 2300 | 100
      2294 |
    - 1150 |  50
      1144 |
    -  920 |  40
       224 |
    -  115 |   5
       109 |
    -   92 |   4
        17   199
```

7. 26 pages
8. **A.** 62 marbles
   **B.** Yes; 13 marbles will be left over.
9. 63 miles
10. 39 packages
11. 43 strips

*Answers and/or discussion are included in the Lesson Guide.

Name ______________________ Date ____________

# Unit 9 Home Practice

**PART 1 Division Practice**

**Solve each problem using paper and pencil. Estimate to see if your answers are reasonable. Explain your estimation strategy for Question A.**

| | |
|---|---|
| A. 5762 ÷ 8 = | B. 1263 ÷ 9 = |
| C. 4691 ÷ 3 = | D. 3189 ÷ 3 = |

**PART 2 Fractions and Decimals**

1. Find a pair of equivalent fractions in each set. You may use a calculator or another strategy. Be prepared to explain your thinking.

| | | | | |
|---|---|---|---|---|
| A. | $\frac{7}{15}$ | $\frac{28}{75}$ | $\frac{79}{160}$ | $\frac{21}{45}$ |
| B. | $\frac{15}{20}$ | $\frac{125}{200}$ | $\frac{3}{5}$ | $\frac{27}{45}$ |
| C. | $\frac{1}{3}$ | $\frac{33}{100}$ | $\frac{4}{5}$ | $\frac{11}{33}$ |
| D. | $\frac{6}{16}$ | $\frac{24}{36}$ | $\frac{36}{112}$ | $\frac{66}{176}$ |

2. Use your calculator to change each fraction to a decimal (to the nearest hundredth). Then change each decimal to a percent.

| | Decimal | Percent |
|---|---|---|
| A. $\frac{4}{5}$ | ______ | ______ |
| B. $\frac{7}{12}$ | ______ | ______ |
| C. $\frac{4}{15}$ | ______ | ______ |





***Discovery Assignment Book* - page 147**

## Discovery Assignment Book (p. 147)

### Home Practice*

### Part 2. Fractions and Decimals

1. A. $\frac{7}{15} = \frac{21}{45}$ B. $\frac{3}{5} = \frac{27}{45}$
   C. $\frac{1}{3} = \frac{11}{33}$ D. $\frac{6}{16} = \frac{66}{176}$
2. A. 0.8, 80% B. 0.58, 58%
   C. 0.27, 27%

Name ______________________ Date ____________

## Estimation and Division

**Estimate each quotient. Tell what strategy you used to make your estimate.**

Example: $22\overline{)834}$

Think:

| | |
|---|---|
| 22 × 10 = | 220 |
| 22 × 20 = | 440 |
| 22 × 30 = | 660 |
| 22 × 40 = | 880 |

←834

Answer: I used multiples of 10. Since 834 is between 22 × 30 = 660 and 22 × 40 = 880, the quotient will be at least 30 but less than 40.

1. $11\overline{)258}$
2. $21\overline{)753}$
3. $32\overline{)568}$
4. $25\overline{)648}$
5. $42\overline{)3253}$
6. $38\overline{)6206}$
7. $50\overline{)792}$
8. $73\overline{)7890}$





***Discovery Assignment Book* - page 153**

## Discovery Assignment Book (p. 153)

### Estimation and Division

For ***Questions 1–8,*** answers and strategies will vary.

1. Between 20 and 30.
2. Between 30 and 40.
3. Between 10 and 20.
4. Between 20 and 30.
5. Between 50 and 100.
6. Between 100 and 200.
7. Between 10 and 20.
8. Between 100 and 200.

*Answers for all the Home Practice in the *Discovery Assignment Book* are at the end of the unit.

## Discovery Assignment Book (p. 155)

### More Estimation and Division

For ***Questions 1–6,*** answers and strategies may vary.

1. Between 40 and 50.
2. Between 100 and 130.
3. Between 100 and 130.
4. Between 300 and 400.
5. Between 50 and 60.
6. Between 250 and 320.

Name ______________________ Date ____________

### More Estimation and Division

**Estimate each quotient. Tell what strategy you used to make your estimate.**

Example: 27 $\overline{)8432}$

Think:

| | |
|---|---|
| 25 × 200 = | 5000 |
| 25 × 300 = | 7500 |
| 25 × 400 = | 10,000 |

← 8432

Possible answer: Use 25 as a convenient number for 27. I tried multiples of 100. Since 8432 is between 25 × 300 and 25 × 400, the quotient is between 300 and 400.

1. 12 $\overline{)497}$
2. 79 $\overline{)9898}$
3. 52 $\overline{)6449}$
4. 26 $\overline{)8970}$
5. 17 $\overline{)874}$
6. 32 $\overline{)9583}$



Division DAB • Grade 5 • Unit 9 • Lesson 2 155

*Discovery Assignment Book* - page 155

# Multiplication Methods

## Lesson Overview

**Estimated Class Sessions**
**2**

Different methods for paper-and-pencil multiplication are discussed in the context of checking a division problem. Lattice multiplication is introduced. Students solve problems involving two-digit by three-digit multiplication.

## Key Content

- Introducing lattice multiplication.
- Multiplying 2 digits × 3 digits using paper-and-pencil methods.
- Comparing multiplication methods.

## Key Vocabulary

- lattice multiplication

## Homework

1. Assign the *Lattice Multiplication Practice* Activity Pages.
2. Assign the Homework section in the *Student Guide*.

# Curriculum Sequence

## Before This Unit

In Unit 2, students explored two methods of paper-and-pencil multiplication—the all-partials method and the compact method. Egyptian multiplication was described in the fourth grade Adventure Book *Phil and Howard's Excellent Egyptian Adventure* in Unit 11.

# Materials List

### Supplies and Copies

| Student | Teacher |
|---|---|
| **Supplies for Each Student** | **Supplies** |
| **Copies** | **Copies/Transparencies** |

*All blackline masters including assessment, transparency, and DPP masters are also on the Teacher Resource CD.*

### Student Books

*Multiplication Methods* (*Student Guide* Pages 299–303)
*Lattice Multiplication Practice* (*Discovery Assignment Book* Pages 157–158)

## Multiplication Methods

**Multiplying with Pencil and Paper**

Mr. Moreno's class decided to make a book of the best short stories that they wrote. They decided to call this book *Life in Fifth Grade.* Mr. Moreno made copies of the book on the school copy machine. He used 9568 sheets of paper. He knows that he used 26 sheets of paper to make each book.

1. How many copies of *Life in Fifth Grade* did Mr. Moreno make?
2. Ana divided the 9568 sheets of paper by 26 and got the answer 368 copies. Is Ana correct? Show how you would check Ana's answer.

Multiplication Methods SG • Grade 5 • Unit 9 • Lesson 3 
299

***Student Guide* - page 299** *(Answers on p. 71)*

Romesh checked Ana's calculation by multiplying. He used the all-partials method to multiply 26 by 368.

$$\begin{array}{r} 368 \\ \times\ 26 \\ \hline 48 \\ 360 \\ 1800 \\ 160 \\ 1200 \\ 6000 \\ \hline 9568 \end{array}$$

3. How did Romesh get the partial product 48?
4. How did Romesh get the partial product 1200?
5. How did Romesh get the partial product 6000?
6. What color is the ones' column shaded?
7. What color is the tens' column shaded?
8. Which column is shaded green and which column is shaded yellow?

**Lattice Multiplication**

Blanca said she knew another way to multiply 368 × 26. She called it **lattice multiplication.** To start the problem, she drew this diagram with 368 across the top and 26 down the right side.

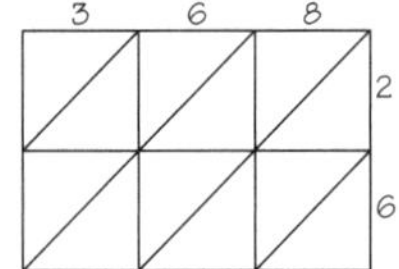


300 SG • Grade 5 • Unit 9 • Lesson 3 Multiplication Methods

***Student Guide* - page 300** *(Answers on p. 71)*

## Teaching the Activity

### Part 1 Multiplying with Pencil and Paper

This lesson discusses several multiplication algorithms. Use the *Multiplication Methods* Activity Pages in the *Student Guide* to guide discussion. Mr. Moreno's class discusses two paper-and-pencil multiplication methods for checking whether $9568 \div 26 = 368$. Ask students to solve $26 \times 368$ with pencil and paper and look for the strategies they devise to solve the problem. If they recall their work with the all-partials method in Unit 2, they may use the strategy shown in the *Student Guide.*

There are a great many strategies students can use. For example, one common strategy is to think of twenty-six as $10 + 10 + 6$, twenty-six 368's is $10 \times 368 + 10 \times 368 + 6 \times 368$. So, the result is:

$$\begin{array}{c} 10 \times 368 = 3680 \\ 10 \times 368 = 3680 \\ 6 \times 368 = 2208 \\ \text{since } 3680 + 3680 + 2208 = 9568 \\ \text{then } 26 \times 368 = 9568 \end{array}$$

In ***Questions 3–8,*** students discuss the all-partials method as a way to compute $26 \times 368$. Previously, students used the all-partials method to multiply two-digit by two-digit and one-digit by multidigit problems. Multiplying two-digit by three-digit numbers is a natural extension. Some students may be familiar with the traditional compact method of multiplying:

$$\begin{array}{r} {\scriptstyle 1\,1} \\ {\scriptstyle 4\,4} \\ 368 \\ \underline{\times\ 26} \\ 2208 \\ \underline{7360} \\ 9568 \end{array}$$

## Part 2 Lattice Multiplication

In the Lattice Multiplication section of the *Multiplication Methods* Activity Pages, Blanca introduces another paper-and-pencil multiplication method. **Lattice multiplication** is really a variation of the all-partials method. The lattice method arranges the partial products in such a way that you do not have to write down the ending zeros. Putting the products in the lattice automatically puts the digits in the correct place value columns. Many students enjoy using this method.

The *Student Guide* shows one example of lattice multiplication, a two-digit times a three-digit number. You can extend the same method for any multiplication problem.

To solve 26 × 368, follow these steps.

Step 1: Draw a 2 by 3 lattice and put the factors across the top and right hand side.

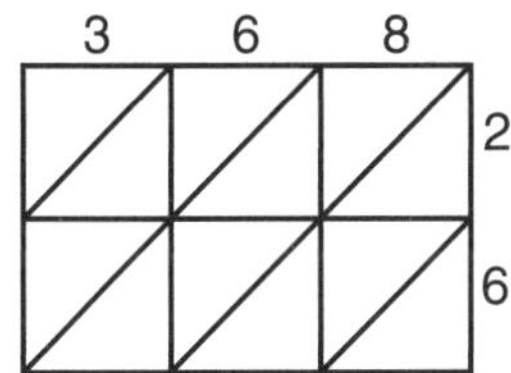


Step 2: Multiply the first partial product and fill it in.

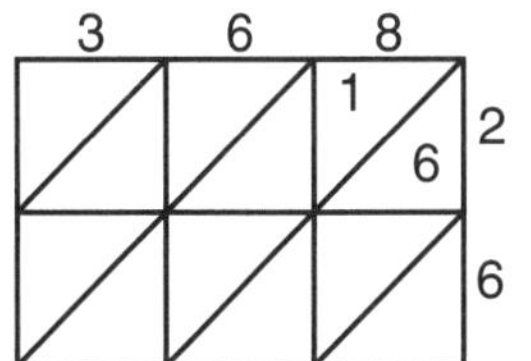


Step 3: Fill in each of the partial products as shown. For example, 8 × 6 = 48, so 48 is entered in the lower right hand corner.

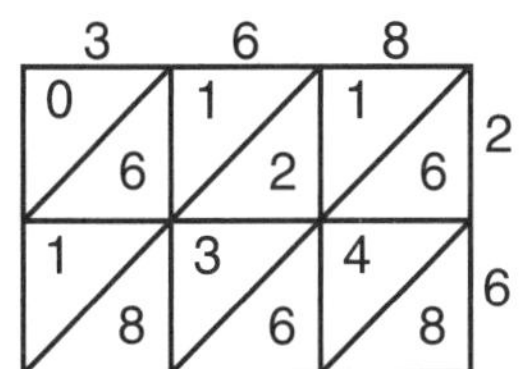


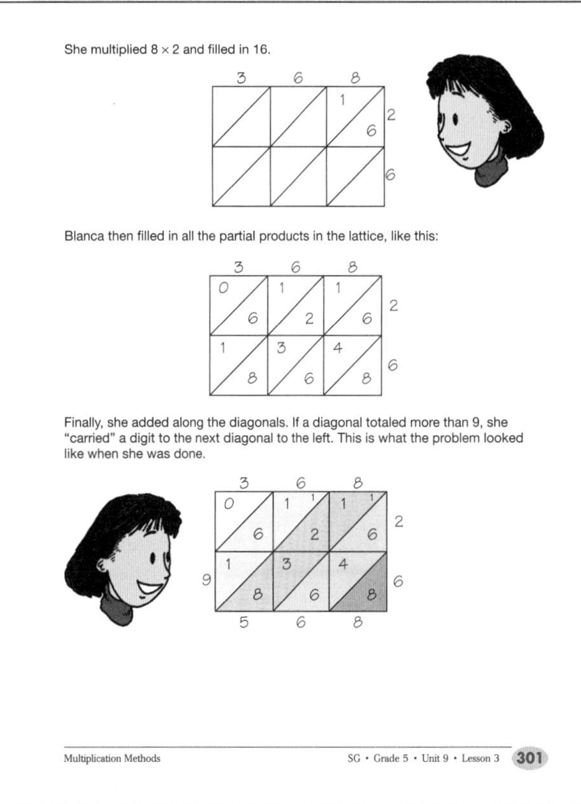

She multiplied 8 × 2 and filled in 16.

Blanca then filled in all the partial products in the lattice, like this:

Finally, she added along the diagonals. If a diagonal totaled more than 9, she "carried" a digit to the next diagonal to the left. This is what the problem looked like when she was done.

Multiplication Methods SG • Grade 5 • Unit 9 • Lesson 3 301

***Student Guide* - page 301**

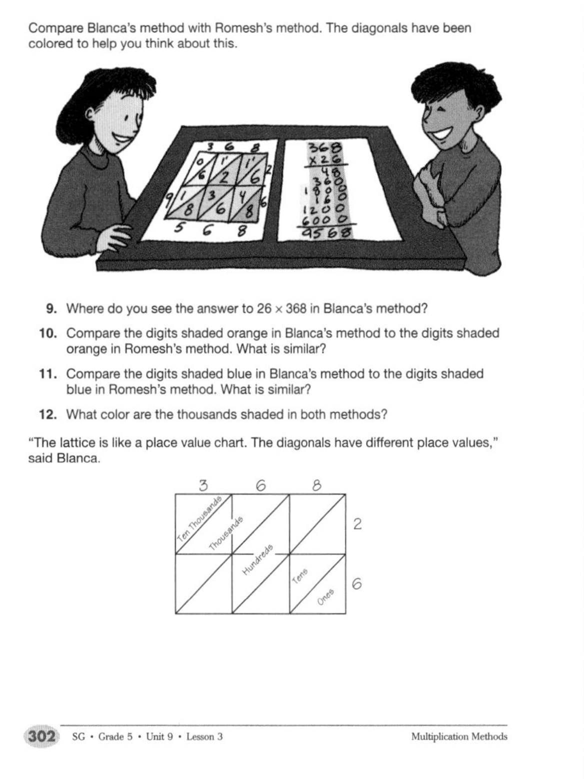

Compare Blanca's method with Romesh's method. The diagonals have been colored to help you think about this.

9. Where do you see the answer to 26 × 368 in Blanca's method?
10. Compare the digits shaded orange in Blanca's method to the digits shaded orange in Romesh's method. What is similar?
11. Compare the digits shaded blue in Blanca's method to the digits shaded blue in Romesh's method. What is similar?
12. What color are the thousands shaded in both methods?

"The lattice is like a place value chart. The diagonals have different place values," said Blanca.



302 SG • Grade 5 • Unit 9 • Lesson 3 Multiplication Methods

***Student Guide* - page 302** *(Answers on p. 72)*

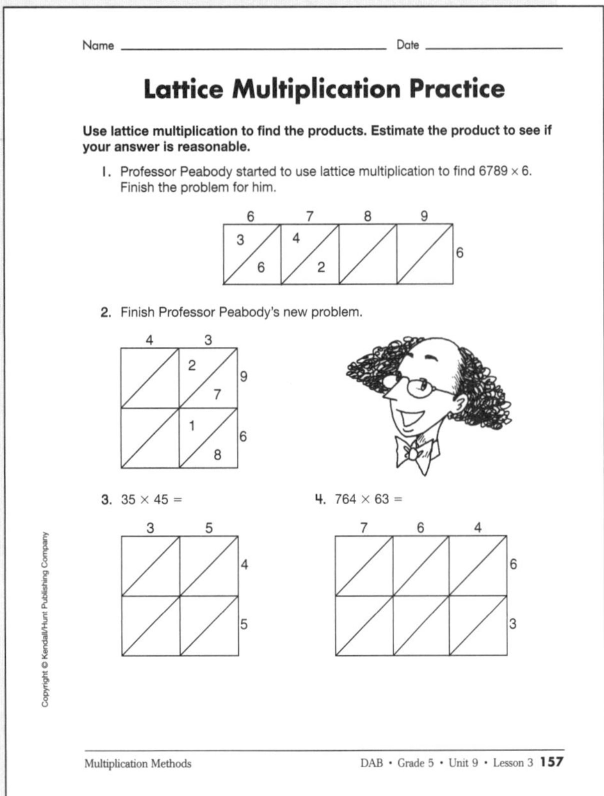

Name ______________________ Date ______________

## Lattice Multiplication Practice

**Use lattice multiplication to find the products. Estimate the product to see if your answer is reasonable.**

1. Professor Peabody started to use lattice multiplication to find 6789 × 6. Finish the problem for him.

2. Finish Professor Peabody's new problem.

3. 35 × 45 =

4. 764 × 63 =

Copyright © Kendall/Hunt Publishing Company

Multiplication Methods DAB • Grade 5 • Unit 9 • Lesson 3 **157**

***Discovery Assignment Book* - page 157** *(Answers on p. 73)*

Name ______________________ Date ______________

**Draw your own lattices for Questions 5 and 6. Then solve the problems.**

5. 28 × 79 =

6. 953 × 57 =

**For Questions 7 and 8, make up two of your own multiplication problems and solve them using lattice multiplication. Check your answer using another method.**

7.

8.

Copyright © Kendall/Hunt Publishing Company

**158** DAB • Grade 5 • Unit 9 • Lesson 3 Multiplication Methods

***Discovery Assignment Book* - page 158** *(Answers on p. 73)*

Step 4: Add the numbers along the diagonal columns. You have to "carry" if you have a sum greater than nine. The product, 9568, is displayed along the left hand and bottom sides of the lattice.

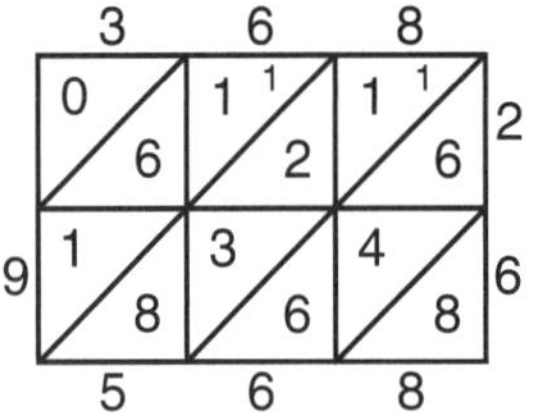


Encourage students to compare the all-partials method to lattice multiplication using ***Questions 9–12*** in the *Student Guide.*

Assign the *Lattice Multiplication Practice* Activity Pages in the *Discovery Assignment Book* for additional practice using lattice multiplication.

### Part 3 Many Ways to Multiply

The Many Ways to Multiply section in the *Student Guide* points out that there are many different correct methods for multiplying numbers using pencil and paper. All methods are based on the idea of breaking up the multiplication problem into groups and computing the groups individually, although this is not always so obvious. You may find that some students will come into your class having learned a different algorithm. If they have a method that works, that's fine. They should continue using their method if it is efficient.

Have students complete ***Questions 13–16*** in the *Student Guide* using two different multiplication algorithms they choose.

## Journal Prompt

Compare all the methods you have used for multiplication. Are some methods better than others? Why? Which method do you like the best?

The Journal Prompt asks students which methods they like the best and why. Encourage students to justify their choices and explain their reasoning, showing examples on the board or overhead. Discuss when it is appropriate to use a calculator and estimation. Calculators are appropriate when speed and accuracy are important. Estimation is appropriate when an exact answer is not necessary or not meaningful. For more background on the *Math Trailblazers* approach to computation and journal writing, see the TIMS Tutor: *Arithmetic* and the TIMS Tutor: *Journals* in the *Teacher Implementation Guide.*

### Many Ways to Multiply

Five of the students worked on the problem 37 × 499. They each used a different method.

"I didn't realize there were so many methods for multiplying," said Romesh.

"Yes," said Jessie. "I learned the compact method from my Dad."

"There are a lot more methods than the ones we have talked about. In some countries children learn even different methods," replied Mr. Moreno. "Most methods are based on the idea that multiplication problems with big numbers can be broken into many multiplications."

**Find the following products in at least two different ways. Discuss with your classmates which methods were most efficient. Which were most reliable?**

**13.** 36 × 502
**14.** 499 × 6
**15.** 53 × 123
**16.** 76 × 804

#### Homework

**Estimate the answers to the following problems. Then show how to find an exact answer using as many methods as you can.**

**1.** 4598 × 5
**2.** 45 × 36
**3.** 201 × 35
**4.** 399 × 32
**5.** 3002 × 50
**6.** Which method of solving these problems do you like the most? Do you think the same method is best for all problems?

***Student Guide* - page 303** *(Answers on p. 72)*

## Homework and Practice

- Assign the *Lattice Multiplication Practice* Activity Pages in the *Discovery Assignment Book* for additional practice.
- Assign the Homework section in the *Student Guide.*

## Assessment

While knowledge of multiplication facts is absolutely essential, there is no need to drill students for speed in using the multiplication algorithm. In any situation where speed is necessary, i.e., where numerous exact answers are required, the technology to solve these problems (namely, calculators and computers) is available. Therefore, we recommend that you avoid assessments containing many multidigit multiplication problems that assess computation speed. A moderate number of problems in which students use any paper-and-pencil method is more appropriate.

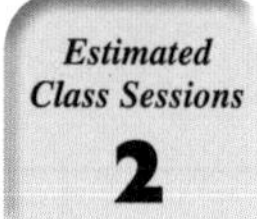
Estimated Class Sessions
2

# At a Glance

## Part 1. Multiplying with Pencil and Paper

1. Students solve 26 × 368 using their own strategies.
2. Read the Multiplying with Pencil and Paper section of the *Multiplication Methods* Activity Pages in the *Student Guide.*
3. Students complete ***Questions 1–8***.

## Part 2. Lattice Multiplication

1. Show students how to do 26 × 368 using lattice multiplication.
2. Read and discuss the Lattice Multiplication section in the *Student Guide.* Compare the all-partials method and lattice multiplication by looking at which digits appear in each place value column. ***(Questions 9–12)***
3. Students complete the *Lattice Multiplication Practice* Activity Pages in the *Discovery Assignment Book.*

## Part 3. Many Ways to Multiply

1. Together, read the Many Ways to Multiply section in the *Student Guide.*
2. Students solve the multiplication problems in ***Questions 13–16*** using at least two methods.
3. Students compare all the methods they use for multiplication by writing a response to the journal prompt.

## Homework

1. Assign the *Lattice Multiplication Practice* Activity Pages.
2. Assign the Homework section in the *Student Guide.*

*Answer Key is on pages 71–73.*

## Notes:

## Student Guide (p. 299)

### Multiplication Methods

1. 368
2. Yes; $368 \times 26 = 9568$

## Multiplication Methods

**Multiplying with Pencil and Paper**

Mr. Moreno's class decided to make a book of the best short stories that they wrote. They decided to call this book *Life in Fifth Grade.* Mr. Moreno made copies of the book on the school copy machine. He used 9568 sheets of paper. He knows that he used 26 sheets of paper to make each book.



1. How many copies of *Life in Fifth Grade* did Mr. Moreno make?
2. Ana divided the 9568 sheets of paper by 26 and got the answer 368 copies. Is Ana correct? Show how you would check Ana's answer.

Multiplication Methods SG • Grade 5 • Unit 9 • Lesson 3 299

***Student Guide* - page 299**

## Student Guide (p. 300)

3. $6 \times 8$
4. $60 \times 20$
5. $300 \times 20$
6. Orange
7. Blue
8. Hundreds' column is colored green and thousands' column is colored yellow.

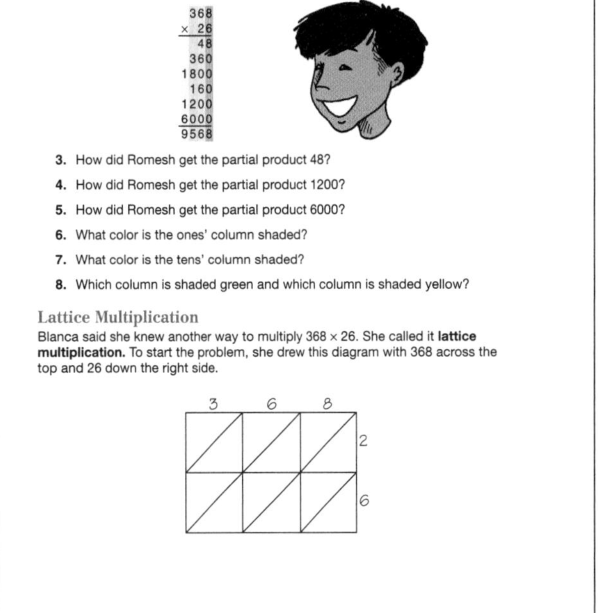

Romesh checked Ana's calculation by multiplying. He used the all-partials method to multiply 26 by 368.



3. How did Romesh get the partial product 48?
4. How did Romesh get the partial product 1200?
5. How did Romesh get the partial product 6000?
6. What color is the ones' column shaded?
7. What color is the tens' column shaded?
8. Which column is shaded green and which column is shaded yellow?

**Lattice Multiplication**

Blanca said she knew another way to multiply 368 × 26. She called it **lattice multiplication.** To start the problem, she drew this diagram with 368 across the top and 26 down the right side.



300 SG • Grade 5 • Unit 9 • Lesson 3 Multiplication Methods

***Student Guide* - page 300**

*Answers and/or discussion are included in the Lesson Guide.

Compare Blanca's method with Romesh's method. The diagonals have been colored to help you think about this.

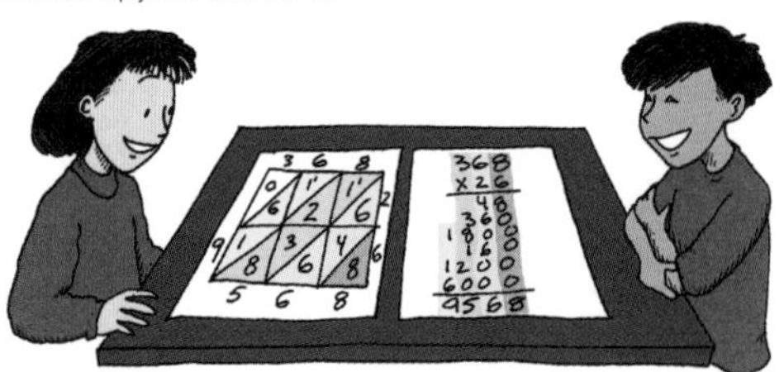

9. Where do you see the answer to 26 × 368 in Blanca's method?
10. Compare the digits shaded orange in Blanca's method to the digits shaded orange in Romesh's method. What is similar?
11. Compare the digits shaded blue in Blanca's method to the digits shaded blue in Romesh's method. What is similar?
12. What color are the thousands shaded in both methods?

"The lattice is like a place value chart. The diagonals have different place values," said Blanca.

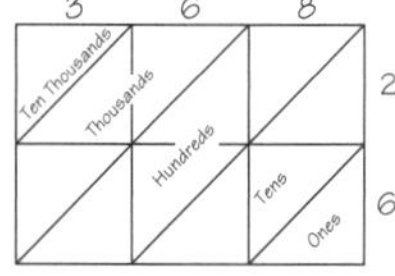


302 SG • Grade 5 • Unit 9 • Lesson 3 Multiplication Methods

*Student Guide* - page 302

## Student Guide (p. 302)

9. Left hand side and bottom of lattice
10. In both methods the digit shaded orange or the ones' digit is the same, 8.
11. In both methods the digits shaded blue or the tens' digits are the same, 4, 6, and 6.
12. Yellow

### Many Ways to Multiply

Five of the students worked on the problem 37 × 499. They each used a different method.

"I didn't realize there were so many methods for multiplying," said Romesh.

"Yes," said Jessie. "I learned the compact method from my Dad."

"There are a lot more methods than the ones we have talked about. In some countries children learn even different methods," replied Mr. Moreno. "Most methods are based on the idea that multiplication problems with big numbers can be broken into many multiplications."

**Find the following products in at least two different ways. Discuss with your classmates which methods were most efficient. Which were most reliable?**

13. 36 × 502
14. 499 × 6
15. 53 × 123
16. 76 × 804

**Estimate the answers to the following problems. Then show how to find an exact answer using as many methods as you can.**

1. 4598 × 5
2. 45 × 36
3. 201 × 35
4. 399 × 32
5. 3002 × 50
6. Which method of solving these problems do you like the most? Do you think the same method is best for all problems?

Multiplication Methods SG • Grade 5 • Unit 9 • Lesson 3 

*Student Guide* - page 303

## Student Guide (p. 303)

For ***Questions 13–16*** methods will vary.

13. 18,072
14. 2994
15. 6519
16. 61,104

### Homework

For ***Questions 1–5,*** answers may vary. One possible estimate is given for each question.

1. 25,000; 22,990
2. 2000; 1620
3. 7000; 7035
4. 12,000; 12,768
5. 150,000; 150,100
6. Answers will vary.

## Discovery Assignment Book (pp. 157–158)

### Lattice Multiplication Practice

1. Answer: 40,734

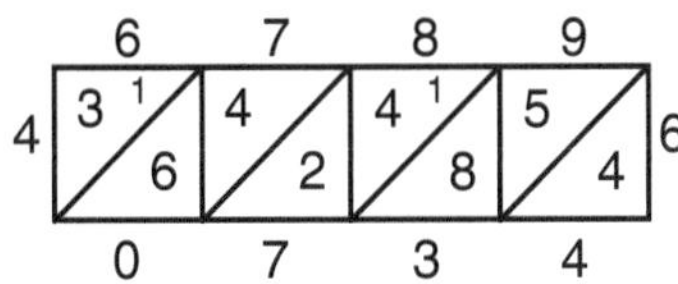

2. Answer: 4128

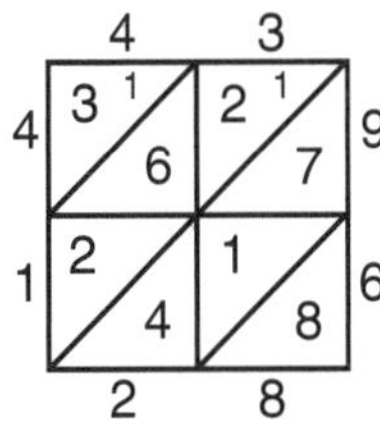

3. Answer: 1575

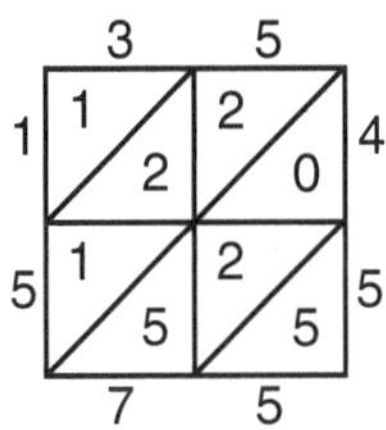

4. Answer: 48,132

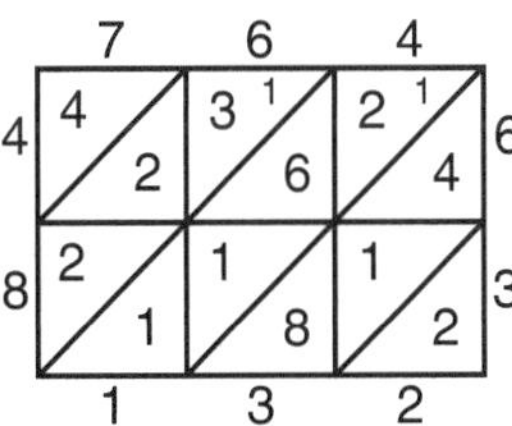

5. Answer: 2212

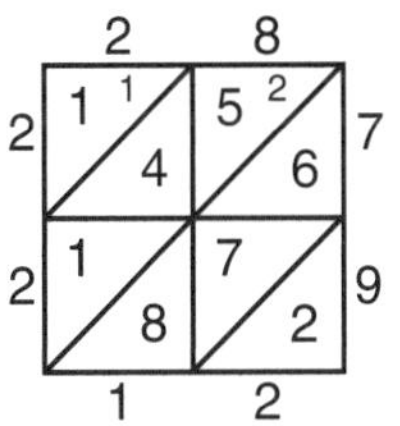

6. Answer: 54,321

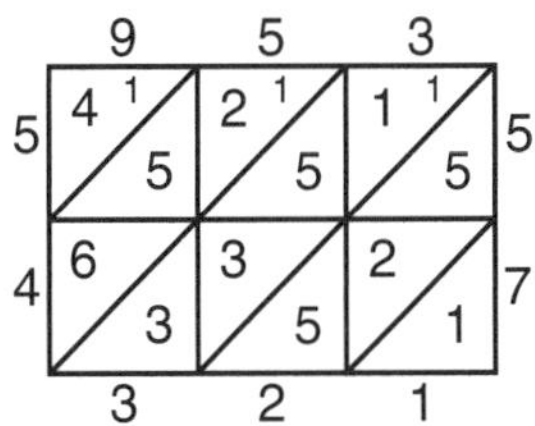

7. Answers will vary. The problem must be a 2-digit by 2-digit multiplication problem.
8. Answers will vary. The problem must be a 3-digit by 2-digit multiplication problem.

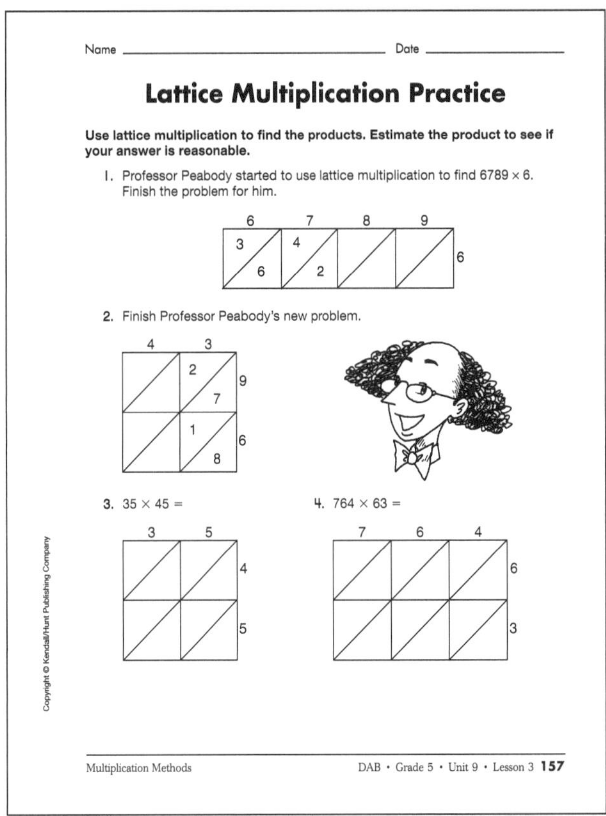

Name ______________________ Date ____________

**Lattice Multiplication Practice**

**Use lattice multiplication to find the products. Estimate the product to see if your answer is reasonable.**

1. Professor Peabody started to use lattice multiplication to find 6789 × 6. Finish the problem for him.

2. Finish Professor Peabody's new problem.

3. 35 × 45 =

4. 764 × 63 =

Copyright © Kendall/Hunt Publishing Company

Multiplication Methods DAB • Grade 5 • Unit 9 • Lesson 3 157

*Discovery Assignment Book* - page 157

Name ______________________ Date ____________

**Draw your own lattices for Questions 5 and 6. Then solve the problems.**

5. 28 × 79 =

6. 953 × 57 =

**For Questions 7 and 8, make up two of your own multiplication problems and solve them using lattice multiplication. Check your answer using another method.**

7.

8.



158 DAB • Grade 5 • Unit 9 • Lesson 3 Multiplication Methods

*Discovery Assignment Book* - page 158

# Understanding Remainders

## Lesson Overview

*Estimated Class Sessions*

**2**

Students interpret remainders in division problems. They complete problems in which a remainder requires rounding the quotient to the next whole number, the remainder is dropped from the answer, and the remainder is the answer to the problem. Students also express quotients as mixed numbers.

### Key Content

- Interpreting remainders in division problems.
- Writing quotients as mixed numbers.
- Solving division problems.

### Math Facts

DPP items K and M review the multiplication and division facts for the 5s and 10s.

### Homework

1. Assign ***Questions 4–9*** on the *Understanding Remainders* Activity Pages.
2. Assign homework ***Questions 1–10*** in the *Student Guide*.
3. Assign Parts 3 and 4 of the Home Practice.

### Assessment

1. Students complete the *Tie Dye T-Shirts* Assessment Page.
2. Use DPP Task N as a quiz.
3. Use the *Observational Assessment Record* to note students' abilities to interpret remainders.

## Curriculum Sequence

### Before This Unit

Students explored remainders to division problems in Lessons 2 and 3 of Unit 4. They worked with mixed numbers and equivalent fractions in Units 3 and 5.

# Materials List

## Supplies and Copies

| Student | Teacher |
|---|---|
| **Supplies for Each Student** | **Supplies** |
| **Copies**<br>• 1 copy of *Tie Dye T-Shirts* per student (*Unit Resource Guide* Page 82) | **Copies/Transparencies** |

*All blackline masters including assessment, transparency, and DPP masters are also on the Teacher Resource CD.*

## Student Books

*Understanding Remainders* (*Student Guide* Pages 304–309)

## Daily Practice and Problems and Home Practice

DPP items K–N (*Unit Resource Guide* Pages 19–21)
Home Practice Parts 3–4 (*Discovery Assignment Book* Pages 148–149)

Note: Classrooms whose pacing differs significantly from the suggested pacing of the units should use the Math Facts Calendar in Section 4 of the *Facts Resource Guide* to ensure students receive the complete math facts program.

## Assessment Tools

*Observational Assessment Record* (*Unit Resource Guide* Pages 11–12)

# Daily Practice and Problems

Suggestions for using the DPPs are on page 80.

### K. Bit: More Fact Practice (URG p. 19)

Find $n$ to make each number sentence true.

A. $n \times 5 = 40$
B. $n \times 7 = 70$
C. $n \div 4 = 5$
D. $80 \div n = 10$
E. $10 \times n = 50$
F. $30 \div 5 = n$
G. $9 \times 10 = n$
H. $15 \div n = 5$
I. $n \times 8 = 80$

### L. Task: *Digits Game:* Addition with Decimals (URG p. 20)

Draw boxes like these on your paper.

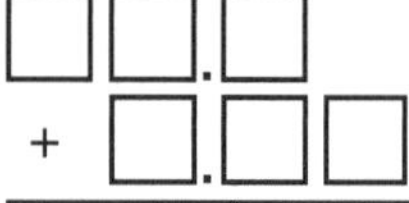

As your teacher or classmate chooses digits from a deck of digit cards, place them in the boxes. Try to make the largest sum. Remember, each digit will be read only once. Once you place a digit, it cannot be moved.

### M. Bit: Multiplying and Dividing by Multiples of Ten (URG p. 20)

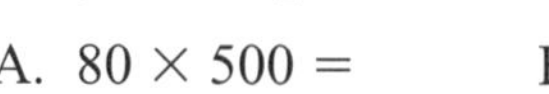

A. $80 \times 500 =$
B. $60 \times 100 =$
C. $20 \times 5000 =$
D. $3000 \div 60 =$
E. $70{,}000 \div 100 =$
F. $4500 \div 90 =$

### N. Task: Operations (URG p. 21)

Use paper and pencil or mental math, not your calculator, to solve these problems. Write any remainders as whole numbers. When you finish a problem, look back to see if your answer is reasonable.

A. $59 \times 14 =$
B. $86 \times 42 =$
C. $409 \times 4 =$
D. $2486 \div 4 =$
E. $2486 \div 14 =$
F. $1067 \div 37 =$

## Teaching the Activity

### Part 1 Understanding Remainders

Review the *Division* Activity Pages in the *Student Guide* for Lesson 2. In this vignette, some students from Mr. Moreno's class are helping to plan a menu for a parent dinner. They decide how many pans of enchilada casserole will be needed by dividing the expected number of people by the number of servings each pan will make. Looking at just the paper-and-pencil computation, students see that the quotient is 12 with a remainder of 5. Ask:

- *How does the remainder in this problem help you decide how many pans of casserole are needed?* (The remainder shows that if they make 12 pans of enchilada casserole, five people will not get any food. As a result, the children must make one more pan of casserole.)

Ask students to open their *Student Guides* to the *Understanding Remainders* Activity Pages. Have small groups complete ***Questions 1–3*** followed by sharing and discussing answers in the large group. For each question, students compute the answer using paper and pencil.

In ***Question 1,*** students decide how many buses are needed to transport a group of children to weekend camp. One way of completing the paper-and-pencil computation using the forgiving method is shown in Figure 12.

$$
\begin{array}{r|l}
\text{5 R43} & \\
63\overline{)\,358} & \\
-315 & 5 \\
\hline
43 &
\end{array}
$$

**Figure 12:** *A paper-and-pencil computation for* ***Question 1***

In this problem, the remainder tells the number of students who will not have a seat if only 5 buses are used. Having a remainder greater than zero tells us that 1 more bus is needed, for a total of 6 buses.

***Question 2*** asks students how many tents they can set up if there are 102 tent stakes and each tent uses 8 stakes. The quotient 12 and remainder 6 tells us that after we set up 12 tents we will still have 6 stakes left over. Since 6 stakes are not enough for another tent, the remainder is dropped from the answer. Only 12 tents can be set up.

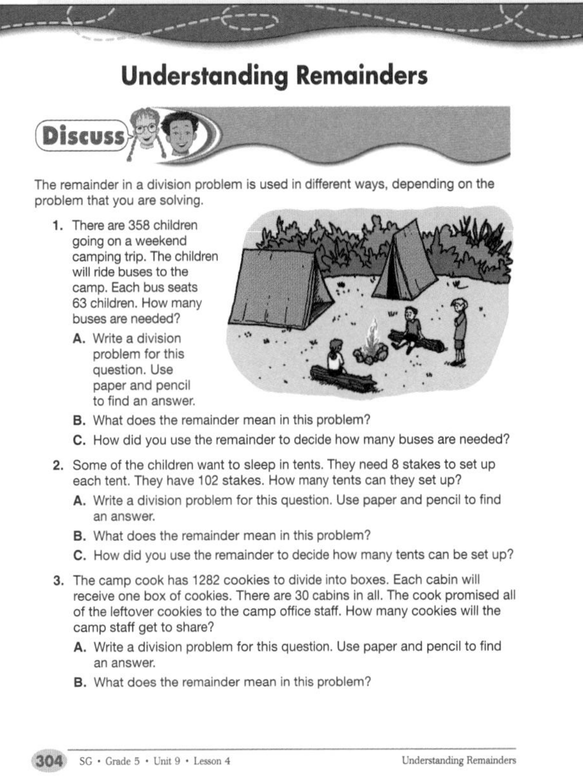

**Understanding Remainders**

**Discuss**

The remainder in a division problem is used in different ways, depending on the problem that you are solving.

1. There are 358 children going on a weekend camping trip. The children will ride buses to the camp. Each bus seats 63 children. How many buses are needed?
   - A. Write a division problem for this question. Use paper and pencil to find an answer.
   - B. What does the remainder mean in this problem?
   - C. How did you use the remainder to decide how many buses are needed?
2. Some of the children want to sleep in tents. They need 8 stakes to set up each tent. They have 102 stakes. How many tents can they set up?
   - A. Write a division problem for this question. Use paper and pencil to find an answer.
   - B. What does the remainder mean in this problem?
   - C. How did you use the remainder to decide how many tents can be set up?
3. The camp cook has 1282 cookies to divide into boxes. Each cabin will receive one box of cookies. There are 30 cabins in all. The cook promised all of the leftover cookies to the camp office staff. How many cookies will the camp staff get to share?
   - A. Write a division problem for this question. Use paper and pencil to find an answer.
   - B. What does the remainder mean in this problem?

304 SG • Grade 5 • Unit 9 • Lesson 4 Understanding Remainders

***Student Guide* - page 304** *(Answers on p. 83)*

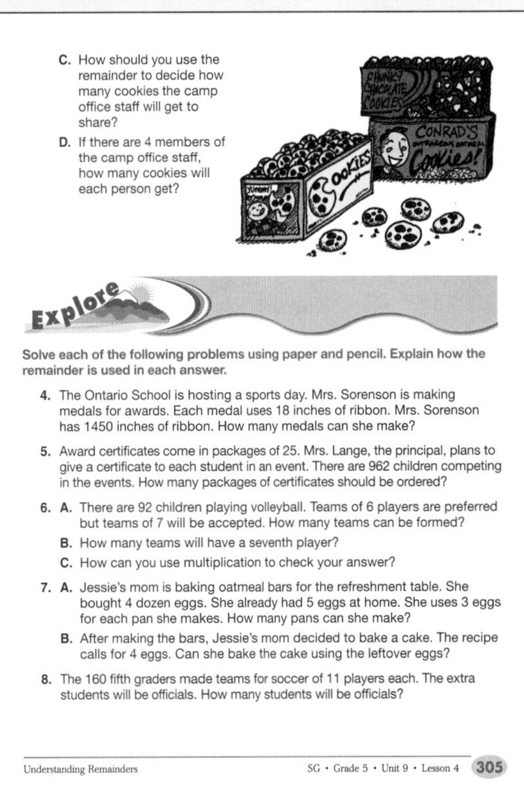

- C. How should you use the remainder to decide how many cookies the camp office staff will get to share?
- D. If there are 4 members of the camp office staff, how many cookies will each person get?



**Explore**

**Solve each of the following problems using paper and pencil. Explain how the remainder is used in each answer.**

4. The Ontario School is hosting a sports day. Mrs. Sorenson is making medals for awards. Each medal uses 18 inches of ribbon. Mrs. Sorenson has 1450 inches of ribbon. How many medals can she make?
5. Award certificates come in packages of 25. Mrs. Lange, the principal, plans to give a certificate to each student in an event. There are 962 children competing in the events. How many packages of certificates should be ordered?
6. A. There are 92 children playing volleyball. Teams of 6 players are preferred but teams of 7 will be accepted. How many teams can be formed?
   - B. How many teams will have a seventh player?
   - C. How can you use multiplication to check your answer?
7. A. Jessie's mom is baking oatmeal bars for the refreshment table. She bought 4 dozen eggs. She already had 5 eggs at home. She uses 3 eggs for each pan she makes. How many pans can she make?
   - B. After making the bars, Jessie's mom decided to bake a cake. The recipe calls for 4 eggs. Can she bake the cake using the leftover eggs?
8. The 160 fifth graders made teams for soccer of 11 players each. The extra students will be officials. How many students will be officials?

Understanding Remainders SG • Grade 5 • Unit 9 • Lesson 4 305

***Student Guide* - page 305** *(Answers on p. 83)*

9. A. At the end of the sports day, 1697 ice cream treats were served to the children and their families. The treats came in boxes of 36. How many boxes of ice cream treats were opened?

B. The leftover ice cream treats were given to the volunteers. How many ice cream treats did they get to share?

**More Remainders**

The answer to a division problem can be written as a whole number and a remainder, or, as a mixed number. A mixed number is a whole number plus a fraction. Depending on the problem, one way may be more useful than another.

Lin and David have 18 graham crackers to split among 8 children. To find out how many graham crackers to give each child, Lin wrote this problem: $\frac{18}{8}$. David wrote this problem: $8\overline{)18}$.

10. How are these two problems the same?

Lin found that $\frac{18}{8}$ equals $2\frac{2}{8}$, or $2\frac{1}{4}$. Each child will receive 2 whole crackers. The two leftover crackers will be divided into 8 equal pieces.

Lin's Solution

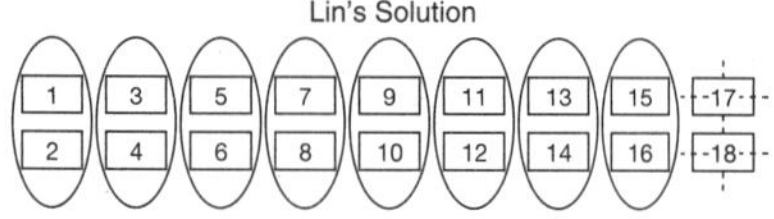


When David solved his problem, he found that 18 divided by 8 is 2 with a remainder of 2 crackers. He wrote his answer as a mixed number: $2\frac{2}{8}$. The fraction $\frac{2}{8}$ in the mixed number $2\frac{2}{8}$ shows that he took the two crackers that were left over and divided them among the eight children.

$$\begin{array}{r|l} \text{2 R2} & \\ 8\overline{)18} & \\ -16 & 2 \\ 2 & \end{array} \quad 2\frac{2}{8}$$

David's Solution

11. A. Where did David get the numbers in this fraction?

B. What information does the numerator give in this fraction?

C. What information does the denominator give in this fraction?

D. Rename $\frac{2}{8}$ using smaller numbers in the numerator and denominator.

E. How many crackers will each child receive?

***Student Guide* - page 306** *(Answers on p. 84)*

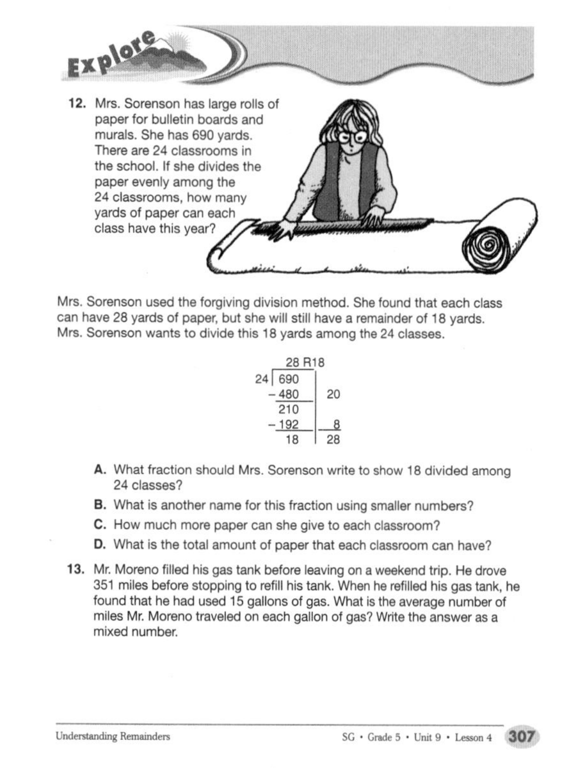

Explore

12. Mrs. Sorenson has large rolls of paper for bulletin boards and murals. She has 690 yards. There are 24 classrooms in the school. If she divides the paper evenly among the 24 classrooms, how many yards of paper can each class have this year?

Mrs. Sorenson used the forgiving division method. She found that each class can have 28 yards of paper, but she will still have a remainder of 18 yards. Mrs. Sorenson wants to divide this 18 yards among the 24 classes.

$$\begin{array}{r|l} \text{28 R18} & \\ 24\overline{)690} & \\ -480 & 20 \\ 210 & \\ -192 & 8 \\ 18 & 28 \end{array}$$

A. What fraction should Mrs. Sorenson write to show 18 divided among 24 classes?

B. What is another name for this fraction using smaller numbers?

C. How much more paper can she give to each classroom?

D. What is the total amount of paper that each classroom can have?

13. Mr. Moreno filled his gas tank before leaving on a weekend trip. He drove 351 miles before stopping to refill his tank. When he refilled his gas tank, he found that he had used 15 gallons of gas. What is the average number of miles Mr. Moreno traveled on each gallon of gas? Write the answer as a mixed number.

Understanding Remainders SG • Grade 5 • Unit 9 • Lesson 4 307

***Student Guide* - page 307** *(Answers on p. 84)*

***Question 3*** asks students to decide how many cookies of the 1282 cookies made will be given to the camp staff. These are the leftovers after the cook distributed the cookies evenly among 30 cabins of children. Once students divide the cookies among the 30 boxes, they will see there are 22 cookies left. Since the camp staff is to receive the leftover cookies, the remainder becomes the answer. ***Question 3D*** asks students to divide the 22 leftover cookies among 4 members of the camp staff. Some students may answer that each staffer will receive 5 cookies with 2 cookies left over, others may answer that each staffer will receive $5\frac{1}{2}$ cookies (dividing the remainder using fractions). Both responses are acceptable, but students should justify their responses.

If students understand how to use remainders, assign ***Questions 4–9*** to be completed independently in class or at home. If students need further guided practice, have students complete these questions in small groups.

## Part 2 More Remainders

This section introduces students to quotients written as mixed numbers. Read the More Remainders section of the *Understanding Remainders* Activity Pages in the *Student Guide.* Students read and discuss the problem of dividing the graham crackers. In ***Question 10,*** $\frac{18}{8}$ and $8\overline{)18}$ are compared. These represent two ways to write 18 divided by 8. Remind students that a fraction is another way to write division, as discussed in Lesson 1. Discuss the diagram in the *Student Guide* showing Lin's solution.

Look at David's solution. Read through the steps that David took to find his solution.

***Question 11A*** asks students why David wrote his quotient as a mixed number. Help students to see that the numerator represents the remainder, while the denominator represents the divisor. ***Questions 11B–11C*** asks students the meaning of the numerator and denominator. The numerator in this fraction tells students the number of leftover crackers. The denominator in this fraction tells students the number of children the crackers are to be divided among.

***Question 11D*** asks students to rename $\frac{2}{8}$. While there are many ways to rename this fraction, we ask them to rename using smaller numbers. Thus their answer should be $\frac{1}{4}$ (i.e., they simplified or reduced the fraction). After answering ***Question 11E,*** students should see that each child will receive $2\frac{1}{4}$ crackers using both Lin's method of dividing and David's method of dividing.

**TIMS Tip**

It is often difficult for students to decide when to write the result of a division as a mixed number. Discuss the types of things that can have fractional parts, for example a quart of milk, and types of things that cannot have fractional parts, such as people or buses.

For ***Question 12*** students should read and discuss the steps that Mrs. Sorenson takes as she computes 690 divided by 24 using the forgiving method. For ***Question 12A,*** students express 18 divided by 24 as a fraction. Make sure students understand that the 18 is the numerator and 24 is the denominator: $\frac{18}{24}$. This fraction is renamed as $\frac{3}{4}$ in ***Question 12B.*** In ***Question 12C,*** this fraction is interpreted to mean that each classroom can have an additional $\frac{3}{4}$ of a yard of paper. In ***Question 12D,*** students find that each classroom will receive $28\frac{3}{4}$ yards of paper this year.

***Questions 13–15*** provide additional practice with quotients expressed as mixed numbers. Students may work in small groups or independently. Provide opportunities for students to discuss their answers and receive feedback. ***Question 15*** asks students to find the number of bricks needed for each row in a walkway. To complete this problem, students will need to express the length of each row in inches. You may need to help students see that 8 feet 6 inches equals $8 \times 12 + 6$ or 102 inches.

**Journal Prompt**

Why are remainders important in a division problem? What information can they give you about your answer? Give examples.

14. The Simply Shirts Company used 608 yards of fabric to make 64 shirts. How much fabric is used in each shirt? Write the answer as a mixed number.
15. Nila is helping her father lay a walkway. They will lay bricks in rows that are each 8 feet 6 inches long. Each brick is 8 inches long. How many bricks will they need for each row in the walkway? Write the answer as a mixed number.

**Homework**

For each of the problems write the answer as a mixed number.

1. Frank and his mother made wooden trains to sell at the yearly craft sale. Over a two-month period, they worked a total of 63 hours and made 18 trains. How many hours did it take to make each train?
2. On a pizza day at Bessie Coleman School, 78 pizzas were divided equally among 24 classrooms. How much pizza did each class receive?
3. The TIMS Candy Company made 60 pounds of Chocos. They put these candies in 24 gift boxes. How many pounds of candy are in each gift box?
4. Romesh is helping his mother build a fence. The fence will be 62 feet 3 inches long. Each fence board is 6 inches wide. How many boards will they need?

5. **A.** 12)507 **B.** 22)825
   **C.** 30)1800 **D.** 24)1260



*Student Guide* - page 308 *(Answers on p. 85)*

Solve each of the problems in Questions 6–10 using paper and pencil.

6. Jackie is working at Billy's Fruit Stand after school. Jackie has to put 2600 apples into bags. Each bag holds three dozen apples. How many bags can she fill?
7. Mrs. Colligan is buying enough lemons so that her third grade class can sell lemonade during lunchtime. The recipe they will use calls for 8 lemons for a pitcher of lemonade. Each pitcher serves 10 people.
   **A.** If they plan to make enough lemonade to serve 480 students and teachers, how many pitchers do they have to make?
   **B.** Eighteen lemons come in a bag. How many bags of lemons should she buy?

8. Billy divides 60 pounds of cherries evenly into 24 boxes. How many pounds of cherries are in each box?
9. Jackie's last job for the day is to divide 725 oranges evenly and put them into 45 bags. Billy told her that she may take any extras home. How many oranges can Jackie take home?

Write any remainders in Question 10 as whole numbers.

10. **A.** 41)8945 **B.** 60)4800 **C.** 68)4912

*Student Guide* - page 309 *(Answers on p. 85)*

Name ______________________ Date ______________

**PART 3 Multiplication and Division Practice**

**Solve the following problems using paper and pencil or mental math. Estimate each answer to be sure it is reasonable.**

A. 63 × 45 = B. 221 ÷ 6 = C. 35 × 29 =

D. 8406 ÷ 23 = E. 0.52 × 0.5 = F. 918 ÷ 54 =

G. 0.83 × 27 = H. 4500 ÷ 15 = I. 12,744 ÷ 68 =



148 DAB • Grade 5 • Unit 9 CONNECTIONS TO DIVISION

***Discovery Assignment Book* - page 148** *(Answers on p. 86)*

Name ______________________ Date ______________

**PART 4 Using Remainders**

**Solve each of the problems below. Show how you solved each one. Be sure to label the numbers you use, especially your answers.**

Four hundred seventy-eight students from Bessie Coleman School are going to the Lizardland Amusement Park for a day.

1. At the Lizardland Amusement Park the roller coaster has 15 cars. Each car holds 4 people. What is the least number of times it will have to run to give all 478 students a ride?
2. Hot pretzels come in packages of 24. The pretzel stand will prepare two pretzels for each student. The workers at the stand will eat the rest of the pretzels. How many will the workers get to eat?
3. The park workers are putting up banners to welcome the school. They use a whole roll of paper that is 200 feet long for the banners. If they make 16 signs, how long will each sign be?
4. The Lizardland train has cars that can carry 18 passengers. If 250 people are riding the train, how many cars will be full?
5. For each of the problems, write any remainder as a mixed number.

   A. 425 ÷ 15 = B. 3500 ÷ 50 = C. 4005 ÷ 18 =



CONNECTIONS TO DIVISION DAB • Grade 5 • Unit 9 149

***Discovery Assignment Book* - page 149** *(Answers on p. 86)*

## Math Facts

DPP items K and M provide multiplication and division practice with the 5s and 10s.

## Homework and Practice

- Use ***Questions 4–9*** from the *Understanding Remainders* Activity Pages as homework.
- Assign homework ***Questions 1–10*** in the *Student Guide.*
- Use DPP Task L to review adding decimals in a game format.
- Assign Parts 3 and 4 of the Home Practice. Part 3 reviews multiplication and division. Part 4 provides practice with interpreting remainders.

*Answers for Parts 3 and 4 of the Home Practice are in the Answer Key at the end of this lesson and at the end of this unit.*

## Assessment

- Use the *Tie Dye T-Shirts* Assessment Page as an assessment.
- Use DPP Task N to assess students' multiplication and division skills.
- Use the *Observational Assessment Record* to note students' abilities to interpret remainders.

### Math Facts and Daily Practice and Problems

DPP items K and M review the multiplication and division facts for the 5s and 10s. Items L and N review decimals, multiplication, and division.

### Part 1. Understanding Remainders

1. Review the opening vignette on the *Division* Activity Pages in the *Student Guide* for Lesson 2.
2. Students complete ***Questions 1–3*** on the *Understanding Remainders* Activity Pages in the *Student Guide.*
3. Provide opportunities in class to discuss the strategies used in ***Questions 1–3***.
4. Students complete ***Questions 4–9*** on the *Understanding Remainders* Activity Pages. These can be used as independent practice, small group work, or homework.

### Part 2. More Remainders

1. Discuss ***Questions 10–11*** from the More Remainders section.
2. Introduce writing a quotient as a mixed number.
3. Students complete ***Question 12*** as additional guided practice.
4. Students complete ***Questions 13–15***.

### Homework

1. Assign ***Questions 4–9*** on the *Understanding Remainders* Activity Pages.
2. Assign homework ***Questions 1–10*** in the *Student Guide.*
3. Assign Parts 3 and 4 of the Home Practice.

### Assessment

1. Students complete the *Tie Dye T-Shirts* Assessment Page.
2. Use DPP Task N as a quiz.
3. Use the *Observational Assessment Record* to note students' abilities to interpret remainders.

***Answer Key is on pages 83–87.***

### Notes:

Name ______________________________ Date ________________

# Tie Dye T-Shirts

**Solve the following problems using a paper-and-pencil method.**

1. Mrs. Sorenson needs 384 white t-shirts to tie dye. If there are 12 t-shirts in a box, how many boxes of t-shirts should Mrs. Sorenson order?

2. Mrs. Sorenson got large bottles of dye from the dye factory. Each bottle will dye 18 t-shirts.

   **A.** How many bottles of dye should Mrs. Sorenson buy to dye all 384 t-shirts?

   **B.** If Mrs. Sorenson buys 19 bottles of dye, how many t-shirts would be left white?

## Student Guide (pp. 304–305)

### Understanding Remainders

1. 6 buses
   - **A.** 358 ÷ 63 = 5 R43. See Figure 12 in Lesson Guide 4 for the paper-and-pencil method.*
   - **B.** The remainder tells the number of students who will not have a seat if only 5 buses are used.
   - **C.** Since the remainder is greater than zero, there should be one more bus, for a total of 6 buses.
2. 12 tents*
   - **A.** 102 ÷ 8 = 12 R6; Methods will vary.
   - **B.** The remainder of 6 means that after setting up 12 tents, there will be 6 stakes left over.
   - **C.** Since 6 stakes are not enough for another tent, the remainder is dropped and only 12 tents can be set up.
3. 22 cookies*
   - **A.** 1282 ÷ 30 = 42 R22
   - **B.** The remainder tells how many cookies are left over after dividing all the cookies evenly among the 30 cabins.
   - **C.** The remainder is the number of cookies left over. Therefore, it is the number of cookies the camp office staff gets to share.
   - **D.** $5\frac{1}{2}$ cookies
4. 80 medals. The remainder 10 inches is not enough for another medal, and therefore, it is dropped.
5. 39 packages. After using 38 packages there will be 12 students left over. Since every student must receive a certificate, one more package should be ordered, for a total of 39 packages.
6. **A.** 15 teams
   - **B.** 2 teams
   - **C.** $13 \times 6 + 2 \times 7 = 92$
7. **A.** 17 pans
   - **B.** No. There are only 2 eggs left over and she needs 4 eggs to bake the cake.
8. 6 students

### Understanding Remainders

**Discuss**

The remainder in a division problem is used in different ways, depending on the problem that you are solving.

1. There are 358 children going on a weekend camping trip. The children will ride buses to the camp. Each bus seats 63 children. How many buses are needed?
   - **A.** Write a division problem for this question. Use paper and pencil to find an answer.
   - **B.** What does the remainder mean in this problem?
   - **C.** How did you use the remainder to decide how many buses are needed?
2. Some of the children want to sleep in tents. They need 8 stakes to set up each tent. They have 102 stakes. How many tents can they set up?
   - **A.** Write a division problem for this question. Use paper and pencil to find an answer.
   - **B.** What does the remainder mean in this problem?
   - **C.** How did you use the remainder to decide how many tents can be set up?
3. The camp cook has 1282 cookies to divide into boxes. Each cabin will receive one box of cookies. There are 30 cabins in all. The cook promised all of the leftover cookies to the camp office staff. How many cookies will the camp staff get to share?
   - **A.** Write a division problem for this question. Use paper and pencil to find an answer.
   - **B.** What does the remainder mean in this problem?

304 SG • Grade 5 • Unit 9 • Lesson 4 — Understanding Remainders

*Student Guide* - page 304

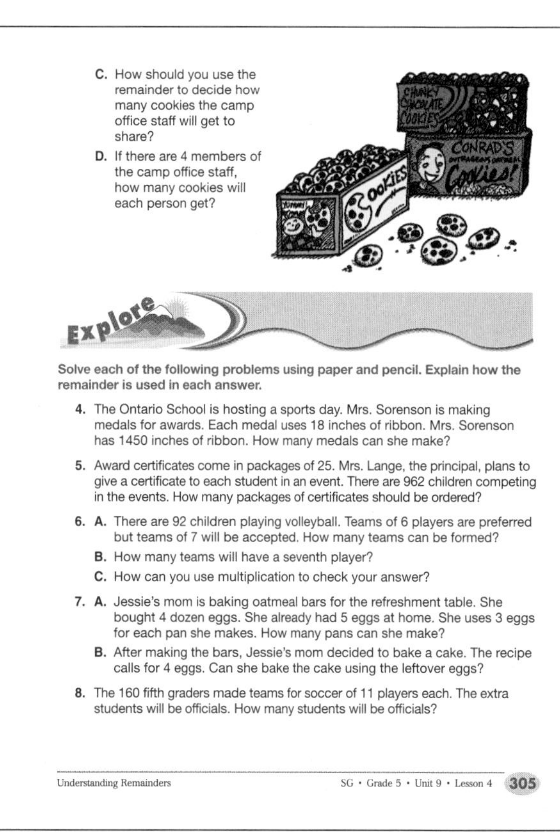

- **C.** How should you use the remainder to decide how many cookies the camp office staff will get to share?
- **D.** If there are 4 members of the camp office staff, how many cookies will each person get?



**Explore**

**Solve each of the following problems using paper and pencil. Explain how the remainder is used in each answer.**

4. The Ontario School is hosting a sports day. Mrs. Sorenson is making medals for awards. Each medal uses 18 inches of ribbon. Mrs. Sorenson has 1450 inches of ribbon. How many medals can she make?
5. Award certificates come in packages of 25. Mrs. Lange, the principal, plans to give a certificate to each student in an event. There are 962 children competing in the events. How many packages of certificates should be ordered?
6. **A.** There are 92 children playing volleyball. Teams of 6 players are preferred but teams of 7 will be accepted. How many teams can be formed?
   - **B.** How many teams will have a seventh player?
   - **C.** How can you use multiplication to check your answer?
7. **A.** Jessie's mom is baking oatmeal bars for the refreshment table. She bought 4 dozen eggs. She already had 5 eggs at home. She uses 3 eggs for each pan she makes. How many pans can she make?
   - **B.** After making the bars, Jessie's mom decided to bake a cake. The recipe calls for 4 eggs. Can she bake the cake using the leftover eggs?
8. The 160 fifth graders made teams for soccer of 11 players each. The extra students will be officials. How many students will be officials?

Understanding Remainders — SG • Grade 5 • Unit 9 • Lesson 4 305

*Student Guide* - page 305

*Answers and/or discussion are included in the Lesson Guide.

9. A. At the end of the sports day, 1697 ice cream treats were served to the children and their families. The treats came in boxes of 36. How many boxes of ice cream treats were opened?

B. The leftover ice cream treats were given to the volunteers. How many ice cream treats did they get to share?

**More Remainders**

The answer to a division problem can be written as a whole number and a remainder, or, as a mixed number. A mixed number is a whole number plus a fraction. Depending on the problem, one way may be more useful than another.

Lin and David have 18 graham crackers to split among 8 children. To find out how many graham crackers to give each child, Lin wrote this problem: $\frac{18}{8}$. David wrote this problem: $8\overline{)18}$.

10. How are these two problems the same?

Lin found that $\frac{18}{8}$ equals $2\frac{2}{8}$, or $2\frac{1}{4}$. Each child will receive 2 whole crackers. The two leftover crackers will be divided into 8 equal pieces.

Lin's Solution

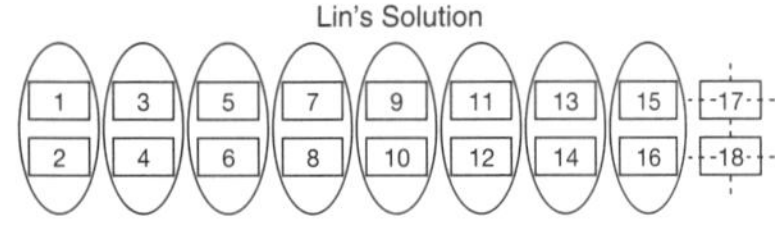


When David solved his problem, he found that 18 divided by 8 is 2 with a remainder of 2 crackers. He wrote his answer as a mixed number: $2\frac{2}{8}$. The fraction $\frac{2}{8}$ in the mixed number $2\frac{2}{8}$ shows that he took the two crackers that were left over and divided them among the eight children.

```
   2 R2
8 | 18  |
  - 16  | 2        2 2/8
     2
```

David's Solution

11. A. Where did David get the numbers in this fraction?

B. What information does the numerator give in this fraction?

C. What information does the denominator give in this fraction?

D. Rename $\frac{2}{8}$ using smaller numbers in the numerator and denominator.

E. How many crackers will each child receive?

SG • Grade 5 • Unit 9 • Lesson 4 Understanding Remainders

***Student Guide* - page 306**

## Student Guide (p. 306)

9. A. 48 boxes

B. 31 ice cream treats

10. These are two different ways of writing the problem 18 divided by 8.*

11. A. The numerator represents the remainder, and the denominator represents the divisor.*

B. The numerator tells the number of leftover crackers.*

C. The denominator tells the number of children the crackers are to be divided among.*

D. $\frac{1}{4}$*

E. $2\frac{1}{4}$

12. Mrs. Sorenson has large rolls of paper for bulletin boards and murals. She has 690 yards. There are 24 classrooms in the school. If she divides the paper evenly among the 24 classrooms, how many yards of paper can each class have this year?

Mrs. Sorenson used the forgiving division method. She found that each class can have 28 yards of paper, but she will still have a remainder of 18 yards. Mrs. Sorenson wants to divide this 18 yards among the 24 classes.

```
    28 R18
24 | 690  |
   - 480  | 20
     210  |
   - 192  |  8
      18  | 28
```

A. What fraction should Mrs. Sorenson write to show 18 divided among 24 classes?

B. What is another name for this fraction using smaller numbers?

C. How much more paper can she give to each classroom?

D. What is the total amount of paper that each classroom can have?

13. Mr. Moreno filled his gas tank before leaving on a weekend trip. He drove 351 miles before stopping to refill his tank. When he refilled his gas tank, he found that he had used 15 gallons of gas. What is the average number of miles Mr. Moreno traveled on each gallon of gas? Write the answer as a mixed number.

Understanding Remainders SG • Grade 5 • Unit 9 • Lesson 4

***Student Guide* - page 307**

## Student Guide (p. 307)

12. A. $\frac{18}{24}$

B. $\frac{3}{4}$

C. $\frac{3}{4}$ yard

D. $28\frac{3}{4}$ yards

13. $23\frac{6}{15} = 23\frac{2}{5}$ miles

*Answers and/or discussion are included in the Lesson Guide.

## Student Guide (p. 308)

14. $9\frac{32}{64}$ or $9\frac{1}{2}$ yds
15. $12\frac{6}{8} = 12\frac{3}{4}$ bricks*

### Homework

1. $3\frac{1}{2}$ hours
2. $3\frac{1}{4}$ pizzas
3. $2\frac{1}{2}$ pounds
4. $124\frac{1}{2}$ boards
5. A. $42\frac{3}{12}$ or $42\frac{1}{4}$
   B. $37\frac{11}{22}$ or $37\frac{1}{2}$
   C. 60
   D. $52\frac{12}{24}$ or $52\frac{1}{2}$

**14.** The Simply Shirts Company used 608 yards of fabric to make 64 shirts. How much fabric is used in each shirt? Write the answer as a mixed number.

**15.** Nila is helping her father lay a walkway. They will lay bricks in rows that are each 8 feet 6 inches long. Each brick is 8 inches long. How many bricks will they need for each row in the walkway? Write the answer as a mixed number.

**Homework**

**For each of the problems write the answer as a mixed number.**

1. Frank and his mother made wooden trains to sell at the yearly craft sale. Over a two-month period, they worked a total of 63 hours and made 18 trains. How many hours did it take to make each train?
2. On a pizza day at Bessie Coleman School, 78 pizzas were divided equally among 24 classrooms. How much pizza did each class receive?
3. The TIMS Candy Company made 60 pounds of Chocos. They put these candies in 24 gift boxes. How many pounds of candy are in each gift box?
4. Romesh is helping his mother build a fence. The fence will be 62 feet 3 inches long. Each fence board is 6 inches wide. How many boards will they need?

5. **A.** $12 \overline{)507}$ **B.** $22 \overline{)825}$
   **C.** $30 \overline{)1800}$ **D.** $24 \overline{)1260}$

308 SG • Grade 5 • Unit 9 • Lesson 4 Understanding Remainders

***Student Guide* - page 308**

## Student Guide (p. 309)

6. 72 bags
7. A. 48 pitchers
   B. 22 bags
8. $2\frac{1}{2}$ lb
9. 5 oranges
10. A. 218 R7
    B. 80
    C. 72 R16

**Solve each of the problems in Questions 6–10 using paper and pencil.**

6. Jackie is working at Billy's Fruit Stand after school. Jackie has to put 2600 apples into bags. Each bag holds three dozen apples. How many bags can she fill?
7. Mrs. Colligan is buying enough lemons so that her third grade class can sell lemonade during lunchtime. The recipe they will use calls for 8 lemons for a pitcher of lemonade. Each pitcher serves 10 people.
   **A.** If they plan to make enough lemonade to serve 480 students and teachers, how many pitchers do they have to make?
   **B.** Eighteen lemons come in a bag. How many bags of lemons should she buy?

8. Billy divides 60 pounds of cherries evenly into 24 boxes. How many pounds of cherries are in each box?
9. Jackie's last job for the day is to divide 725 oranges evenly and put them into 45 bags. Billy told her that she may take any extras home. How many oranges can Jackie take home?

**Write any remainders in Question 10 as whole numbers.**

10. **A.** $41 \overline{)8945}$ **B.** $60 \overline{)4800}$ **C.** $68 \overline{)4912}$

Understanding Remainders SG • Grade 5 • Unit 9 • Lesson 4 

***Student Guide* - page 309**

*Answers and/or discussion are included in the Lesson Guide.

Name ______________________ Date ______________

**PART 3 Multiplication and Division Practice**

**Solve the following problems using paper and pencil or mental math. Estimate each answer to be sure it is reasonable.**

A. $63 \times 45 =$ B. $221 \div 6 =$ C. $35 \times 29 =$

D. $8406 \div 23 =$ E. $0.52 \times 0.5 =$ F. $918 \div 54 =$

G. $0.83 \times 27 =$ H. $4500 \div 15 =$ I. $12{,}744 \div 68 =$



148 DAB • Grade 5 • Unit 9 CONNECTIONS TO DIVISION

***Discovery Assignment Book* - page 148**

## Discovery Assignment Book (p. 148)

### Home Practice*

### Part 3. Multiplication and Division Practice

A. 2835

B. 36 R5

C. 1015

D. 365 R11

E. 0.26

F. 17

G. 22.41

H. 300

I. 187 R28

Name ______________________ Date ______________

**PART 4 Using Remainders**

**Solve each of the problems below. Show how you solved each one. Be sure to label the numbers you use, especially your answers.**

Four hundred seventy-eight students from Bessie Coleman School are going to the Lizardland Amusement Park for a day.

1. At the Lizardland Amusement Park the roller coaster has 15 cars. Each car holds 4 people. What is the least number of times it will have to run to give all 478 students a ride?
2. Hot pretzels come in packages of 24. The pretzel stand will prepare two pretzels for each student. The workers at the stand will eat the rest of the pretzels. How many will the workers get to eat?
3. The park workers are putting up banners to welcome the school. They use a whole roll of paper that is 200 feet long for the banners. If they make 16 signs, how long will each sign be?
4. The Lizardland train has cars that can carry 18 passengers. If 250 people are riding the train, how many cars will be full?
5. For each of the problems, write any remainder as a mixed number.

   A. $425 \div 15 =$ B. $3500 \div 50 =$ C. $4005 \div 18 =$



CONNECTIONS TO DIVISION DAB • Grade 5 • Unit 9 149

***Discovery Assignment Book* - page 149**

## Discovery Assignment Book (p. 149)

### Part 4. Using Remainders

1. 8 runs
2. 4 pretzels
3. 12.5 feet or $12\frac{1}{2}$ feet
4. 13 cars
5. A. $28\frac{5}{15}$ or $28\frac{1}{3}$

   B. 70

   C. $222\frac{9}{18}$ or $222\frac{1}{2}$

*Answers for all the Home Practice in the *Discovery Assignment Book* are at the end of the unit.

## Unit Resource Guide (p. 82)

### Tie Dye T-Shirts

1. 32 boxes

$$\begin{array}{r|l} & 32 \\ 12 \overline{)\ 384} & \\ -360 & 30 \\ \hline 24 & \\ -24 & 2 \\ \hline 0 & 32 \end{array}$$

2. **A.** 22 bottles **B.** 42 t-shirts

Name ______________________ Date ______________

### Tie Dye T-Shirts

**Solve the following problems using a paper-and-pencil method.**

1. Mrs. Sorenson needs 384 white t-shirts to tie dye. If there are 12 t-shirts in a box, how many boxes of t-shirts should Mrs. Sorenson order?

2. Mrs. Sorenson got large bottles of dye from the dye factory. Each bottle will dye 18 t-shirts.
   **A.** How many bottles of dye should Mrs. Sorenson buy to dye all 384 t-shirts?
   **B.** If Mrs. Sorenson buys 19 bottles of dye, how many t-shirts would be left white?





*Unit Resource Guide* **- page 82**

# Calculator Strategies: Division

## Lesson Overview

*Estimated Class Sessions*

1

Students explore using a calculator to divide larger numbers and money. They develop strategies for finding whole number remainders using calculators.

## Key Content

- Using a calculator to divide larger numbers.
- Using a calculator to divide money.
- Finding a whole number remainder using a calculator.
- Estimating quotients.

## Homework

1. Assign homework ***Questions 1–10*** in the *Student Guide*.
2. Assign Part 5 of the Home Practice.

## Assessment

1. Use homework ***Questions 1*** and ***9*** in the *Student Guide* as an assessment.
2. Use the *Observational Assessment Record* to note students' abilities to use a calculator to solve division problems.

# Materials List

## Supplies and Copies

| Student | Teacher |
|---|---|
| **Supplies for Each Student**<br>• calculator | **Supplies** |
| **Copies** | **Copies/Transparencies** |

*All blackline masters including assessment, transparency, and DPP masters are also on the Teacher Resource CD.*

## Student Books

*Calculator Strategies: Division* (*Student Guide* Pages 310–313)

## Daily Practice and Problems and Home Practice

DPP items O–P (*Unit Resource Guide* Pages 21–22)
Home Practice Part 5 (*Discovery Assignment Book* Page 150)

Note: Classrooms whose pacing differs significantly from the suggested pacing of the units should use the Math Facts Calendar in Section 4 of the *Facts Resource Guide* to ensure students receive the complete math facts program.

## Assessment Tools

*Observational Assessment Record* (*Unit Resource Guide* Pages 11–12)

# Daily Practice and Problems

Suggestions for using the DPPs are on page 93.

### O. Bit: Estimate the Products (URG p. 21)

Estimate the products. Be prepared to share how you estimated.

A. $4.2 \times 53 =$　　B. $0.63 \times 0.18 =$
C. $0.25 \times 119 =$　　D. $19 \times 81.56 =$
E. $2.09 \times 3.982 =$　　F. $66 \times 9.09 =$

### P. Task: *Digits Game:* Subtraction with Decimals (URG p. 22)

Draw boxes like these on your paper.

$$\begin{array}{r} \square\square.\square \\ -\ \square.\square\square \\ \hline \end{array}$$

As your teacher or classmate chooses digits from a deck of digit cards, place them in the boxes. Try to make the largest difference. Remember, each digit will be read only once. Once you place a digit, it cannot be moved.

## Calculator Strategies: Division

Think about this division problem: 29 $\overline{)42{,}601}$

1. A. Why is using a calculator a good method for finding the answer to this problem?
   B. Use estimation to decide if the quotient is in the 100s, the 1000s, or the 10,000s.
   C. Here is a set of keystrokes you can use on your calculator to find an answer to this division problem: [42601] [÷] [29] [=]. Use your calculator to solve this problem. Is your answer reasonable based on your estimate?

Money

2. The Parent Teacher Organization gave Mrs. Sorenson $1140 to share among the 24 classrooms for extra art supplies. First, she used a paper-and-pencil method to divide the money. She found that she could give each classroom $47.00, but that would leave a remainder of $12.00.

```
      47 R12
24 | 1140  |
    - 960  | 40
      180  |
    - 168  |  7
       12    47
```

Next, she used her calculator to divide the money among the classrooms.

A. What keystrokes can she use to find an answer to this division problem?
B. Use your calculator to decide how much money each classroom should receive.
C. What do the numbers to the left of the decimal point mean?
D. What do the numbers to the right of the decimal point mean?
E. Why is a calculator a good tool for dividing money?

 SG • Grade 5 • Unit 9 • Lesson 5 Calculator Strategies: Division

***Student Guide* - page 310** *(Answers on p. 95)*

## Teaching the Activity

When students divide larger numbers, they should use calculators to find the quotient. This is a more efficient method than paper-and-pencil procedures. Students need to practice using their calculators so they are comfortable with the keystrokes. They also need to practice estimating to see if their answers are reasonable.

### Content Note

For this lesson we assume students are using calculators that have the correct order of operations, but do not necessarily have features that will display quotients with integer remainders or as mixed numbers. Work with students so they take advantage of features on their calculators to solve problems as efficiently as possible.

**Order of Operations on Calculators.** See the Unit 4 Lesson 5 Lesson Guide for information on how to determine if a calculator has the correct order of operations. If your students do not have calculators with this feature, you will need to help them enter the steps in multistep calculations to get the correct answers.

**Integer Division on Calculators.** Some calculators include two choices for division. One set of keystrokes will produce a decimal. Another set of keystrokes will display a quotient with a whole number remainder.

**Converting Decimals to Fractions.** Some scientific calculators will change decimals to fractions. Students can use this feature to change decimal quotients to mixed numbers.

Ask students to turn to the *Calculator Strategies: Division* Activity Pages in their *Student Guides.* ***Question 1*** asks students why using a calculator is a good method for dividing these larger numbers. Students may respond with the following comments:

- It will save time.
- You save space on your paper when you use a calculator.
- It is quicker than using paper and pencil.

Ask students what problems might arise when using a calculator. Student responses might include:

- The calculator is only as accurate as the person using it. In other words, if you do not enter the correct keystrokes, your answer will not be correct.
- It is sometimes harder to interpret remainders.

In ***Question 1B,*** students estimate the size of the quotient for the problem $29 \overline{)42{,}601}$. To estimate, students need to decide if the quotient will be in the 100s, 1000s, or 10,000s. It might be helpful to organize their thoughts using a chart as shown in Figure 13.

| | |
|---|---|
| 29 × 100 = | 2900 |
| 29 × 1000 = | 29,000 |
| 29 × 10,000 = | 290,000 |

**Figure 13:** *A chart for estimating the size of this quotient*

Since 42,601 is between 29,000 (29 × 1000) and 290,000 (29 × 10,000) the quotient will be at least 1000 but less than 10,000. This means that the quotient will be in the 1000s.

Show students the keystrokes they can use to divide 42,601 by 29. See Figure 14. Make sure students understand that they key in the dividend first, in this case 42,601.

**Figure 14:** *Keystrokes for 42,601 ÷ 29 =*

After finding the solution to this problem using their calculators, students should confirm that the quotient, 1469, is between 1000 and 10,000.

***Question 2*** leads students through a problem of dividing money. Students compare a paper-and-pencil method with the calculator method. In ***Question 2A,*** students identify the keystrokes used to find the quotient using the calculator. See Figure 15.

**Figure 15:** *Keystrokes for 1140 ÷ 24 =*

In ***Question 2C,*** students should identify the numbers to the left of the decimal point in the quotient as the number of dollars each class will receive.

In ***Question 2D,*** they should identify the numbers to the right of the decimal as the number of cents each class will receive. Explain to students that the calculator displays 0.50 as 0.5. Make sure students do not interpret that as 5 cents. Remind them that 0.5 is half of a dollar and that 5 cents is 5 hundredths of a dollar or 0.05.

**Use a calculator to solve these problems. List your keystrokes, and tell what the numbers to the left and to the right of the decimal point mean.**

3. A school spent $2489 to replace 76 science books. What was the cost of each book?
4. The Tasty Pizzeria served 52 large cheese pizzas in one evening. They calculated a total of $650 on the sale of these pizzas. How much did each pizza cost?

5. Three students earned a total of $5.00 washing cars. If they split the money evenly, how much will each student receive?

### Whole Number Remainders

6. A. Jackie and Jessie are dividing cookies into boxes for a bake sale. They have 231 cookies, and they are putting 12 into each box. Use your calculator to divide 231 by 12.
   B. What does the number to the left of the decimal point tell you?
   C. What does the number to the right of the decimal point tell you?
   D. Jessie and Jackie fill 19 boxes with cookies. How many cookies have they put in boxes?

To find the number of leftover cookies, Jackie first found 12 × 19 = 228. This means 228 cookies have been packed. To find the number of cookies remaining, Jackie computed 231 – 228 = 3 cookies.

Calculator Strategies: Division SG • Grade 5 • Unit 9 • Lesson 5 

***Student Guide* - page 311** *(Answers on p. 95)*

**Use a calculator to solve these problems. Show your operations with number sentences. Tell what the numbers to the left and to the right of the decimal point mean. Give whole number remainders with your answer.**

7. The Happy Day Bakery made 542 muffins on Monday.
   A. If they package 2 dozen (24) muffins per box, how many full boxes of muffins did they package?
   B. How many muffins did not get packaged?
8. Penny and Pete's Pencil Company made 38,664 pencils. They packaged them in boxes of 144 pencils.
   A. How many full boxes can they package?
   B. How many pencils will be left over?

**For Questions 1–4, estimate the size of each quotient. Use your calculator to find the answer to each division problem. Write each remainder as a whole number.**

Example: $38\overline{)10{,}051}$ = 264.5 = 264 R19

1. $44\overline{)23{,}375}$ 2. $52\overline{)150{,}000}$ 3. $39\overline{)164{,}754}$ 4. $15\overline{)8925}$

**Use your calculator to solve the following problems. Write your remainder as a whole number.**

5. David has collected 1385 different stamps. He wants to organize them in a book.
   A. If he puts 20 stamps on each page, how many full pages will he use?
   B. How many stamps will be left?

 SG • Grade 5 • Unit 9 • Lesson 5 Calculator Strategies: Division

***Student Guide* - page 312** *(Answers on p. 96)*

In ***Question 2E,*** students identify the advantages of using a calculator to solve this problem. One advantage is that the calculator gives the remainder as a decimal that they can easily read as cents, while the paper-and-pencil method gives the remainder as leftover whole dollars.

Students practice solving more problems involving money in ***Questions 3–5.*** In ***Question 5,*** remind students to give their answer in dollars and cents. Note that 5 ÷ 3 = 1.6666667. Each student will get $1.66 and two cents will be left over.

In ***Question 6,*** students develop strategies for finding the whole number remainder when they use a calculator to divide. In ***Question 6A,*** students use their calculators to divide 231 by 12. They should see 19.25 on their displays after completing the problem. For ***Question 6B,*** students tell what the number to the left of the decimal stands for in this problem. This number tells the number of boxes of cookies Jessie and Jackie can fill for the bake sale. The number to the right of the decimal point is the remainder. In this case, it tells you that you will have 0.25 of a box of cookies remaining ***(Question 6C).*** Discuss:

- *Suggest strategies for finding the number of cookies remaining.* (Remind students they can multiply to check their answers to division problems.)

Three possible strategies:

1. Multiply 19 by 12 to find out how many cookies the girls used to fill the boxes: 19 × 12 = 228 cookies. Then subtract to find how many cookies are left: 231 − 228 = 3 cookies. This number (3) is the whole number remainder.
2. Some students may also remember that .25 is equal to $\frac{1}{4}$. Since there are 12 cookies in a whole box, they can solve $\frac{1}{4}$ of 12 to find 3 as the whole number remainder.
3. Multiply 0.25 × 12 = 3.

***Questions 7–8*** provide additional practice using a calculator to divide. These problems can be assigned as independent or small group practice.

If students have calculators that will display whole number remainders, help them take advantage of this feature to solve problems more efficiently.

## Homework and Practice

- ***Questions 1–10*** in the Homework section of *Calculator Strategies: Division* Activity Pages provide independent practice. Students will need a calculator to complete these problems. Remind students to check their calculators at home for the correct order of operations.
- DPP Bit O provides practice estimating the product of two decimals.
- Assign Part 5 of the Home Practice that includes multistep word problems requiring interpretation of remainders.

*Answers for Part 5 of the Home Practice are in the Answer Key at the end of this lesson and at the end of this unit.*

## Assessment

- Use Homework ***Questions 1*** and ***9*** to assess students' abilities to use the calculator accurately to divide larger numbers and numbers involving money.
- Use the *Observational Assessment Record* to note students' abilities to use a calculator to solve division problems.

## Extension

Practice subtraction with decimals in a game format using DPP item P. You will need *Digit Cards* to play this game.

**6.** Irma is cutting ribbon for a craft project. Each piece must be 16 inches long. She has 508 inches of ribbon.

**A.** How many 16-inch pieces can she cut?

**B.** How many inches of ribbon will be left?

**Use your calculator to solve these problems. Explain any remainders.**

**7.** Mrs. Morgan is a civil engineer. Her job is to plan a bike path around the new park. She needs to decide how many lights she will need along the path. Mrs. Morgan knows that there must be a light every 120 feet. How many lights will she need if the path is 12 miles long? (*Hint:* There are 5280 feet in 1 mile.)

**8.** Crystal Clear window washers washed some large windows on a skyscraper for $3500. If they washed 56 windows on the skyscraper, how much did the company charge to wash each window?

**9.** Perky's Plentiful Peanuts purchased 28 pounds of peanuts from a proprietor for $46.76. How much did Perky's Plentiful Peanuts pay per pound of peanuts?

**10.** Perky's Plentiful Peanuts puts 24 peanuts in a package. Pat, the packer, packaged 1375 peanuts. She ate the leftover peanuts. How many peanuts did she eat?

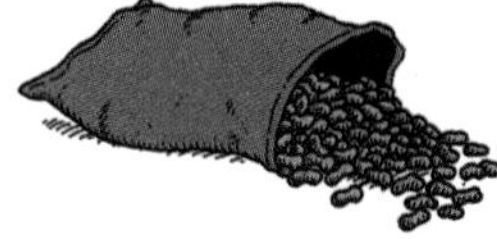

Calculator Strategies: Division SG • Grade 5 • Unit 9 • Lesson 5 313

***Student Guide* - page 313** *(Answers on p. 96)*

Name ______________________ Date ______________

**PART 5 Solving Problems**

**Choose an appropriate method to solve each of the following problems. For each question, you may choose to use paper and pencil, mental math, or a calculator. Use a separate sheet of paper to explain how you solved each problem. (*Hint:* Drawing a picture may help you solve some of the problems.)**

1. Penny's Pencil Company donated a case of pencils to Bessie Coleman Elementary School. The case contains 48 packs of pencils. Each pack contains 24 pencils. The principal wants to divide the pencils equally among 30 classrooms. How many pencils will each classroom receive? How many pencils will be left over for the office?
2. Mr. Moreno is putting together blank research journals for the fifth grade. Each journal needs 7 sheets of paper. Mr. Moreno has 2 packages of paper to use for the journals. How many journals can he make if one package of paper has 144 sheets?
3. The school is sponsoring a cultural fair. The fifth graders are arranging tables and chairs for a refreshment area at the fair. Half of the tables will seat 8 people. Half of the tables will seat 6 people. They have 112 chairs. How many of each kind of table will they set up?
4. One of the classes is serving burritos at the cultural fair. They will use 3 ounces of cheese on each burrito. How many burritos can they make if they have 5 pounds of cheese? (1 pound = 16 ounces)
5. During the cultural fair a group of students will demonstrate an Irish dance. There are 130 chairs available for the audience. The chairs are arranged into 8 equal rows. How many chairs are in each row? How many extra chairs will there be?
6. **A.** At the end of the fair, one group of students found that they served 384 egg rolls. The egg rolls came in boxes of 18. How many boxes of egg rolls did they need?
   **B.** The extra egg rolls were given to the volunteers. How many egg rolls did the volunteers get to share?
   **C.** If each volunteer got the same number of egg rolls and there were 12 volunteers, how many egg rolls did each volunteer get?
7. **A.** Mr. Moreno took 78 pictures at the cultural fair. He wanted to arrange the pictures in an album. Each page of his album holds 8 pictures. How many pages of his album can he completely fill?
   **B.** How many pages will he have to use in all?



150 DAB • Grade 5 • Unit 9 CONNECTIONS TO DIVISION

***Discovery Assignment Book* - page 150** *(Answers on p. 97)*

Estimated Class Sessions

1

# At a Glance

## Math Facts and Daily Practice and Problems

DPP items O–P review estimation and subtraction with decimals.

## Teaching the Activity

1. Use ***Question 1*** on the *Calculator Strategies: Division* Activity Pages to begin a discussion about calculator use.
2. Review strategies for estimating the size of a quotient.
3. Students use calculators to divide large numbers involving money and discuss remainders. ***(Questions 2–5)***
4. Students develop strategies for finding whole number remainders using calculators. ***(Questions 6–8)***

## Homework

1. Assign homework ***Questions 1–10*** in the *Student Guide.*
2. Assign Part 5 of the Home Practice.

## Assessment

1. Use homework ***Questions 1*** and ***9*** in the *Student Guide* as an assessment.
2. Use the *Observational Assessment Record* to note students' abilities to use a calculator to solve division problems.

## Extension

Play the game in DPP item P.

*Answer Key is on pages 95–97.*

## Notes:

## Student Guide (p. 310)

### Calculator Strategies: Division

1.* **A.** Answers will vary. Students might say it will save time, you don't need as much space on your paper, or it is more accurate.

**B.** 1000s

**C.** 1469

2. **A.** [1140] [÷] [24] [=]*

**B.** $47.50

**C.** 47 whole dollars*

**D.** 50¢ per classroom*

**E.** Answers will vary. The remainder is a decimal they can read as cents.*

### Calculator Strategies: Division

Think about this division problem: 29 $\overline{)42{,}601}$

1. **A.** Why is using a calculator a good method for finding the answer to this problem?
   **B.** Use estimation to decide if the quotient is in the 100s, the 1000s, or the 10,000s.
   **C.** Here is a set of keystrokes you can use on your calculator to find an answer to this division problem: [42601] [÷] [29] [=]. Use your calculator to solve this problem. Is your answer reasonable based on your estimate?

**Money**

2. The Parent Teacher Organization gave Mrs. Sorenson $1140 to share among the 24 classrooms for extra art supplies. First, she used a paper-and-pencil method to divide the money. She found that she could give each classroom $47.00, but that would leave a remainder of $12.00.

```
    47 R12
24 | 1140
   - 960  | 40
     180  |
   - 168  |  7
      12    47
```

Next, she used her calculator to divide the money among the classrooms.

**A.** What keystrokes can she use to find an answer to this division problem?
**B.** Use your calculator to decide how much money each classroom should receive.
**C.** What do the numbers to the left of the decimal point mean?
**D.** What do the numbers to the right of the decimal point mean?
**E.** Why is a calculator a good tool for dividing money?

310 SG • Grade 5 • Unit 9 • Lesson 5 Calculator Strategies: Division

*Student Guide* - page 310

## Student Guide (p. 311)

3. [2489] [÷] [76] [=], $32.75, 32 whole dollars and 75¢ for each book

4. [650] [÷] [52] [=], $12.50, 12 dollars and 50¢ per pizza

5. [5.00] [÷] [3] [=], $1.66, 1 dollar and 66¢ for each student with two pennies remaining*

6.* **A.** 19.25

**B.** 19 whole boxes of cookies

**C.** 0.25 or $\frac{1}{4}$ of one box is filled

**D.** 228 cookies

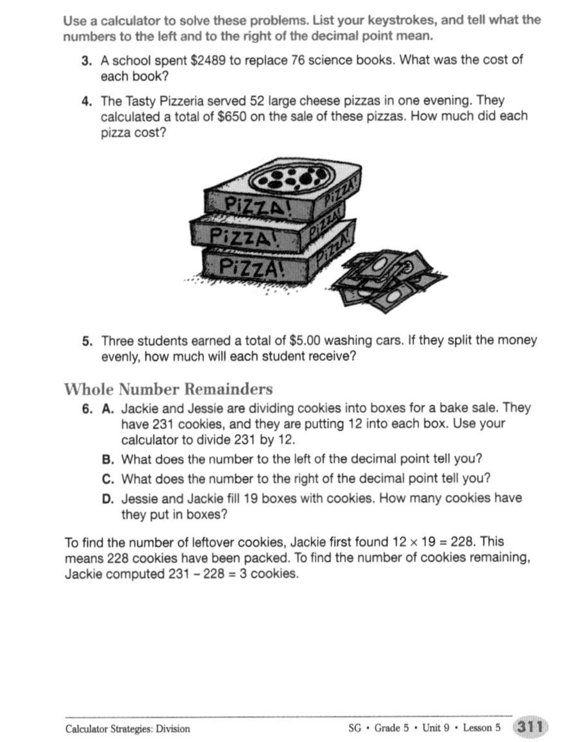

Use a calculator to solve these problems. List your keystrokes, and tell what the numbers to the left and to the right of the decimal point mean.

3. A school spent $2489 to replace 76 science books. What was the cost of each book?
4. The Tasty Pizzeria served 52 large cheese pizzas in one evening. They calculated a total of $650 on the sale of these pizzas. How much did each pizza cost?



5. Three students earned a total of $5.00 washing cars. If they split the money evenly, how much will each student receive?

**Whole Number Remainders**

6. **A.** Jackie and Jessie are dividing cookies into boxes for a bake sale. They have 231 cookies, and they are putting 12 into each box. Use your calculator to divide 231 by 12.
   **B.** What does the number to the left of the decimal point tell you?
   **C.** What does the number to the right of the decimal point tell you?
   **D.** Jessie and Jackie fill 19 boxes with cookies. How many cookies have they put in boxes?

To find the number of leftover cookies, Jackie first found 12 × 19 = 228. This means 228 cookies have been packed. To find the number of cookies remaining, Jackie computed 231 – 228 = 3 cookies.

Calculator Strategies: Division SG • Grade 5 • Unit 9 • Lesson 5 311

*Student Guide* - page 311

*Answers and/or discussion are included in the Lesson Guide.

**Use a calculator to solve these problems. Show your operations with number sentences. Tell what the numbers to the left and to the right of the decimal point mean. Give whole number remainders with your answer.**

7. The Happy Day Bakery made 542 muffins on Monday.
   - **A.** If they package 2 dozen (24) muffins per box, how many full boxes of muffins did they package?
   - **B.** How many muffins did not get packaged?
8. Penny and Pete's Pencil Company made 38,664 pencils. They packaged them in boxes of 144 pencils.
   - **A.** How many full boxes can they package?
   - **B.** How many pencils will be left over?

## Homework

**For Questions 1–4, estimate the size of each quotient. Use your calculator to find the answer to each division problem. Write each remainder as a whole number.**

Example: $38\overline{)10,051}$ 264.5 = 264 R19

**1.** $44\overline{)23,375}$ **2.** $52\overline{)150,000}$ **3.** $39\overline{)164,754}$ **4.** $15\overline{)8925}$

**Use your calculator to solve the following problems. Write your remainder as a whole number.**

5. David has collected 1385 different stamps. He wants to organize them in a book.
   - **A.** If he puts 20 stamps on each page, how many full pages will he use?
   - **B.** How many stamps will be left?

312 SG • Grade 5 • Unit 9 • Lesson 5 Calculator Strategies: Division

*Student Guide* - page 312

6. Irma is cutting ribbon for a craft project. Each piece must be 16 inches long. She has 508 inches of ribbon.
   - **A.** How many 16-inch pieces can she cut?
   - **B.** How many inches of ribbon will be left?

**Use your calculator to solve these problems. Explain any remainders.**

7. Mrs. Morgan is a civil engineer. Her job is to plan a bike path around the new park. She needs to decide how many lights she will need along the path. Mrs. Morgan knows that there must be a light every 120 feet. How many lights will she need if the path is 12 miles long? (*Hint:* There are 5280 feet in 1 mile.)

8. Crystal Clear window washers washed some large windows on a skyscraper for $3500. If they washed 56 windows on the skyscraper, how much did the company charge to wash each window?
9. Perky's Plentiful Peanuts purchased 28 pounds of peanuts from a proprietor for $46.76. How much did Perky's Plentiful Peanuts pay per pound of peanuts?
10. Perky's Plentiful Peanuts puts 24 peanuts in a package. Pat, the packer, packaged 1375 peanuts. She ate the leftover peanuts. How many peanuts did she eat?

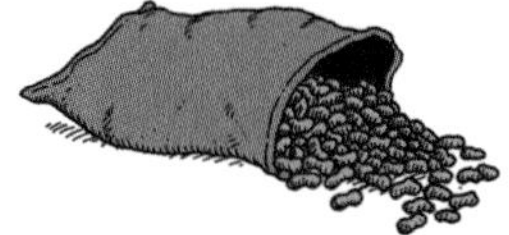

Calculator Strategies: Division SG • Grade 5 • Unit 9 • Lesson 5 313

*Student Guide* - page 313

## Student Guide (pp. 312–313)

**7. A.** 22 full boxes; 542 ÷ 24 = 22.58333 (or R14). The numbers to the left of the decimal show that 22 boxes were completely filled. The numbers to the right of the decimal show that only part of another box will be filled.

**B.** 14 muffins did not get packaged. 24 × 22 = 528; 542 − 528 = 14

**8. A.** 268 full boxes; 38,664 ÷ 144 = 268.5 (or R72). The numbers to the left of the decimal show that 268 boxes will be completely filled. The numbers to the right of the decimal show that only part of another box will be filled.

**B.** 72 pencils; 144 × 268 = 38,592; 38,664 − 38,592 = 72

### Homework

Estimates for ***Questions 1–4*** will vary. One answer is given.

**1.** 500; 531 R11
**2.** 3000; 2884 R32
**3.** 4000; 4224 R18
**4.** 600; 595
**5. A.** 69 full pages
**B.** 5 stamps
**6. A.** 31 pieces
**B.** 12 inches
**7.** 528 lights
**8.** $62.50
**9.** $1.67
**10.** 7 peanuts

## Discovery Assignment Book (p. 150)

### Home Practice*

### Part 5. Solving Problems

1. There is a total of 1152 pencils. Each classroom will get 38 pencils. 12 pencils will be left over for the office.
2. 41 journals. There will be one sheet of paper left over.
3. 8 of each table.
4. 26 burritos
5. 16 rows 2 chairs left over
6. **A.** 22 boxes
   **B.** 6 egg rolls
   **C.** $\frac{1}{2}$ an egg roll
7. **A.** 9 pages
   **B.** 10 pages

Name ______________________ Date ______________

**PART 5** **Solving Problems**

**Choose an appropriate method to solve each of the following problems. For each question, you may choose to use paper and pencil, mental math, or a calculator. Use a separate sheet of paper to explain how you solved each problem. (*Hint:* Drawing a picture may help you solve some of the problems.)**

1. Penny's Pencil Company donated a case of pencils to Bessie Coleman Elementary School. The case contains 48 packs of pencils. Each pack contains 24 pencils. The principal wants to divide the pencils equally among 30 classrooms. How many pencils will each classroom receive? How many pencils will be left over for the office?
2. Mr. Moreno is putting together blank research journals for the fifth grade. Each journal needs 7 sheets of paper. Mr. Moreno has 2 packages of paper to use for the journals. How many journals can he make if one package of paper has 144 sheets?
3. The school is sponsoring a cultural fair. The fifth graders are arranging tables and chairs for a refreshment area at the fair. Half of the tables will seat 8 people. Half of the tables will seat 6 people. They have 112 chairs. How many of each kind of table will they set up?
4. One of the classes is serving burritos at the cultural fair. They will use 3 ounces of cheese on each burrito. How many burritos can they make if they have 5 pounds of cheese? (1 pound = 16 ounces)
5. During the cultural fair a group of students will demonstrate an Irish dance. There are 130 chairs available for the audience. The chairs are arranged into 8 equal rows. How many chairs are in each row? How many extra chairs will there be?
6. **A.** At the end of the fair, one group of students found that they served 384 egg rolls. The egg rolls came in boxes of 18. How many boxes of egg rolls did they need?
   **B.** The extra egg rolls were given to the volunteers. How many egg rolls did the volunteers get to share?
   **C.** If each volunteer got the same number of egg rolls and there were 12 volunteers, how many egg rolls did each volunteer get?
7. **A.** Mr. Moreno took 78 pictures at the cultural fair. He wanted to arrange the pictures in an album. Each page of his album holds 8 pictures. How many pages of his album can he completely fill?
   **B.** How many pages will he have to use in all?





***Discovery Assignment Book* - page 150**

*Answers for all the Home Practice in the *Discovery Assignment Book* are at the end of the unit.

# Grass Act

## Lesson Overview

*Estimated Class Sessions*

**2**

This assessment is an open-response problem that asks students to estimate the number of blades of grass in a specified area. Students use sampling to make their estimates. First students use a vignette in the *Student Guide* as a context for working with a group to develop a plan for solving the problem. Then students collect data and use it to solve the problem and write about their solutions.

## Key Content

- Solving open-response problems and communicating solution strategies.
- Developing number sense for large numbers.
- Collecting and using data to solve problems.
- Averaging.
- Measuring area.
- Solving problems involving multiplication.
- Using the *Solving, Knowing,* and *Telling* Rubrics to self-assess problem-solving skills.

## Math Facts

DPP items Q and S practice the facts for the 5s and 10s.

## Homework

Assign the Journal Prompt for homework.

## Assessment

1. Use DPP Challenge T as an assessment of concepts learned in this unit.
2. Transfer appropriate documentation from the Unit 9 *Observational Assessment Record* to students' *Individual Assessment Record Sheets*.

# Curriculum Sequence

## Before This Unit

### Sampling

In Unit 1 students used sampling procedures in the labs *Eyelets* and *Searching the Forest*. In Unit 2 students read the Adventure Book *Sand Reckoning*. In the story, Archimedes used sampling to estimate the number of grains of sand it would take to fill the universe. You may want to review this story before beginning this assessment activity.

### Open-response problems

Students solved several open-response problems during the year. In Unit 2, students used number patterns and estimation to complete the problem *Stack Up* in Lesson 9. In Unit 8, they analyzed data and then used the data to make predictions in Lesson 4 *Florence Kelley's Report*.

## After This Unit

### Open-response problems

Students will continue to solve open-response problems in labs in succeeding units. Unit 11 Lesson 7 and Unit 16 Lesson 5 also provide opportunities to solve open-response problems and communicate solution strategies.

# Materials List

## Supplies and Copies

| Student | Teacher |
|---|---|
| **Supplies for Each Student**<br>• calculator<br>• 3" by 5" index card<br>**Supplies for Each Student Group**<br>• scissors<br>• ruler | **Supplies**<br>• a large grassy area or piece of sod, nylon netting, window screen, or large beach towel |
| **Copies**<br>• 1 copy of *Grass Act Questions* per student (*Unit Resource Guide* Page 113) | **Copies/Transparencies**<br>• 1 copy of *TIMS Multidimensional Rubric* (*Teacher Implementation Guide,* Assessment section)<br>• 1 transparency or poster of Student Rubrics: *Solving, Knowing,* and *Telling,* optional (*Teacher Implementation Guide,* Assessment section) |

*All blackline masters including assessment, transparency, and DPP masters are also on the Teacher Resource CD.*

## Student Books

*Grass Act* (*Student Guide* Page 314)
Student Rubric: *Knowing* (*Student Guide* Appendix A and Inside Back Cover), optional
Student Rubric: *Solving* (*Student Guide* Appendix B and Inside Back Cover)
Student Rubric: *Telling* (*Student Guide* Appendix C and Inside Back Cover), optional

## Daily Practice and Problems and Home Practice

DPP items Q–T (*Unit Resource Guide* Pages 22–24)

Note: Classrooms whose pacing differs significantly from the suggested pacing of the units should use the Math Facts Calendar in Section 4 of the *Facts Resource Guide* to ensure students receive the complete math facts program.

## Assessment Tools

*Observational Assessment Record* (*Unit Resource Guide* Pages 11–12)
*TIMS Multidimensional Rubric* (*Teacher Implementation Guide,* Assessment section)
*Individual Assessment Record Sheet* (*Teacher Implementation Guide,* Assessment section)

# Daily Practice and Problems

Suggestions for using the DPPs are on page 111.

**Q. Bit: Dividing by Multiples of Ten** (URG p. 22)

A. 9000 ÷ 100 =
B. 45,000 ÷ 900 =
C. 20,000 ÷ 2 =
D. 350 ÷ 70 =
E. 250,000 ÷ 500 =
F. 30,000 ÷ 30 =

**R. Task: Thinking about Remainders** (URG p. 23)

1. You are dividing a number by 6 and at the end of the problem your remainder is 7. What does that mean?
2. Make a list of the possible remainders you can have when you finish dividing a number by 8.

**S. Bit: Reviewing Division Facts: 5s and 10s** (URG p. 23)

A. 45 ÷ 5 =
B. 25 ÷ 5 =
C. 10 ÷ 2 =
D. 60 ÷ 10 =
E. 40 ÷ 8 =
F. 30 ÷ 3 =
G. 20 ÷ 5 =
H. 80 ÷ 10 =
I. 30 ÷ 6 =
J. 35 ÷ 5 =
K. 15 ÷ 3 =
L. 50 ÷ 10 =
M. 70 ÷ 10 =
N. 90 ÷ 9 =
O. 40 ÷ 4 =
P. 20 ÷ 2 =
Q. 100 ÷ 10 =

**T. Challenge: Remainders** (URG p. 24)

1. Solve each of the following problems. Each one has a remainder. Write the quotient three ways: with a whole number remainder, as a mixed number, and as a decimal.
   A. 6 ÷ 4 =
   B. 19 ÷ 4 =
   C. 49 ÷ 4 =
2. Choose one of the problems. Write 3 different stories for the problem showing how you might use each of the three types of quotients.

## Before the Activity

This assessment activity asks students to estimate the number of blades of grass in a given area. Choose an appropriate section of the school yard or nearby park. For the number of blades of grass to be in the millions, you need an area greater than 20 sq yd. (This estimate is based on student-collected data. If a square inch of grass has about 40 blades of grass, then 20 sq yd of grass will have about 1,000,000 blades of grass. The number of blades of grass per square inch will vary from lawn to lawn.)

If your school does not have access to grass, four alternatives are outlined below.

1. If you have a grassy lawn to use as your representative area, but prefer not to take students outside, consider bringing a piece of sod into the classroom. The children can do their sampling with the sod and the experience can be nearly as rich. Give students the area of the section of lawn in square yards or square feet, then ask them to estimate the number of blades of grass in the lawn. Alternatively, students can solve this problem:
   - *If the classroom floor were covered with grass, how many blades of grass would there be in the classroom?*

You may choose to use one of the three man-made alternatives in this activity: estimating the number of loops on a towel, holes in a screen, or holes in nylon netting. However, the numbers will not be quite as large or the magnitude of the amounts as visually accessible. To actually show a number well into the millions, you need many feet of towel, screen, or netting.

2. Nylon netting is an inexpensive alternative for this activity. Found in most fabric stores, one yard of netting that is 72 inches wide has about 200,000 holes. Five yards of netting provides a good, concrete look at just over 1 million holes. Ask:
   - *How many holes are in the nylon netting?*
3. Another alternative, though slightly more costly, is window screen. A piece of screen $7\frac{1}{2}$ feet square will have about 1 million holes. If you choose to use window screen for this activity, use plastic or fiberglass screen instead of metal to prevent accidental cuts. Ask:
   - *How many holes are in the screen?*

4. A final alternative is a towel. The loops that make up the pile are a little trickier to count, but possible. A typical hand towel measuring 15 inches by 20 inches will have about 100,000 loops. Ask:
   - *How many loops are on the towel?*

This Lesson Guide is written as if the activity will be completed using grass on a lawn. If you choose to use an alternative activity, adjust your lesson plans accordingly.

## Teaching the Activity

### Part 1 Developing a Plan

Read the *Grass Act* Activity Page in the *Student Guide* so students understand the context of the problem. After reading the exchange between Manny and Felicia, students work together in groups to develop a plan that will determine the number of grass blades in a lawn ***(Question 1).***

**Grass Act**

Manny: I can't believe how long it took me to cut the grass in our yard Saturday. There must be a zillion blades of grass there.

Felicia: There's no such thing as a zillion.

Manny: I know. It's just a way of saying there's a whole lot. Still, I wonder how many blades of grass are in my yard? It would be really interesting to find out. I wonder how we can.

1. Think about how Manny and Felicia can estimate the number of blades of grass in the yard. Work with your group to develop a plan to solve this problem.
2. Record your group's plan. Use the Student Rubric: *Solving* to help you as you write your plan.

314 SG • Grade 5 • Unit 9 • Lesson 6 Grass Act

***Student Guide* - page 314**

Before students begin working on their plans, review the rubrics you will use to assess their work. We recommend that you assess students' written plans using the *Solving* Rubric. Encourage students to use the student rubrics as self-assessment tools as they write their plans. You can also review the Student Rubrics: *Knowing* and *Telling*. Then assess their knowledge of skills and concepts and their abilities to communicate mathematically using those dimensions.

Although students develop their plans collaboratively with their groups, each student should record his or her plan independently ***(Question 2).*** Groups should work without consulting you and rely instead on their group members to help them with questions. If a group needs additional help from you to get started, note this so you can include this information in your evaluation.

You may want to remind students about the Adventure Book *Sand Reckoning* at this time.

Student plans should include:

- finding the total area of the lawn;
- counting the blades of grass in several sample areas from the lawn;
- finding the average number of blades of grass in the samples; and
- using this average to estimate the number of blades of grass in the larger area.

If students have difficulty devising a plan, review the sampling strategy used in *Sand Reckoning.* Ask students to think about how they can use sampling to estimate the number of blades of grass in a given area. Encourage students to choose an appropriate sample size such as a square inch.

### Part 2 Solving the Problem

Once each group completes the questions in the *Student Guide,* distribute the *Grass Act Questions* Assessment Page from the *Unit Resource Guide.* Identify the questions students must answer. They should work in their groups to collect the data, then independently to calculate their estimates and explain their strategies.

Students may choose different procedures for isolating a sample. One possible method is to use a note card with a square-inch hole removed to isolate a square inch "sample" of grass to count.

Once students solve the problem and complete their writing, review their work for possible revisions. Then score their work using the dimensions of the rubric you chose.

Students can add their papers to their collection folders for possible inclusion in their portfolios. Encourage students to compare their work on this problem with similar problems from earlier in the year to see their growth in problem solving in fifth grade. They can compare this work to problems such as *Stack Up* from Unit 2 and *Florence Kelley's Report* from Unit 8.

To assist you in scoring student work, we list specific questions for each dimension of the *TIMS Multidimensional Rubric.*

#### Solving

- Did students clearly understand the relationship between the elements of this problem? For example, did they understand the relationship between the total area of the lawn and the sample size?
- Did students use efficient problem-solving strategies? For example, did they choose an appropriate sample size? Did they choose a practical method for converting square inches to square feet (or square yards)?
- Did they understand that an exact answer is not possible and choose efficient strategies to find an estimate?
- Did students organize their information? For example, did they record the counts from each sample? Did they organize their work using pictures or tables?

**TIMS Tip**

While the total area of the lawn will likely be measured in square feet or square yards, the sample size probably will be measured in square inches. Therefore, students will need to convert between units of measure. If you have to prompt students to make the conversions, note it so you can take this into consideration during your evaluation.

- Did they relate this problem to previously encountered mathematics? For example, did they use sampling as an estimation technique? Did they take multiple samples to get a more accurate estimate? Did they use averages as a way to "even out" the numbers in their samples?
- Did students work until they reached a solution? Did they solve the problem a second way as a check on their first solution?
- Did they look back to see if their solutions were reasonable?

**Knowing**

- Did students understand the task's mathematical concepts and apply them accurately? For example, did they know they needed to convert between square yards and square inches? Did they know how to use a sampling technique? Did they take multiple samples?
- Did students translate between words, pictures, symbols, and real situations? For example, did they draw a picture of the regions they sampled along with the whole area? Did they clearly explain their procedures in symbols and words?
- Did students use the mathematical tools accurately? For example, did they use their calculators correctly? Did they measure correctly?
- Did students use their knowledge of mathematics to solve this problem? For example, did they find the average accurately? Did they convert between square yards and square inches correctly? Did they compute accurately when estimating the number of blades of grass in the total area?

**Telling**

- Were students' explanations clear and concise? Did they include each step of their plans? Did they clearly explain how they estimated the total number of blades of grass?
- Did students present supporting arguments for their conclusions? For example, did they show more than one way to arrive at the solution?
- Did students use pictures, symbols, or tables to clarify the explanation? Did they use correct number sentences in their explanations? Did they include diagrams or tables?
- Did students use correct terminology? For example, did students use square inches or square feet when discussing the area?

Sample student work follows. Student A estimated the total number of blades of grass in a portion of a playground. Student B estimated the number of holes in a window screen. Their work was scored using all three dimensions of the *TIMS Multidimensional Rubric.*

**Student A's work:**

STEP1: first we found a grassy spot to start at.
STEP2: Then we used a toothpick to pull up the blades of grass and counted them with it.
STEP3. Then we measured the section mrs. mitteree marked off. (we used yards.)
STEP4: Then we wrote down the data we collected and did all of our math. we used multiplaction and additions (11yrd and 16" and 10yrds and 21".)

STEPS IN OUR MATH,
first we did 10 times 36 because there are 36" in a yrd. then we added 21" to that because there was still 21" left over and that was 381. then we multiplyed 11 times 36 because there are 36" in a yrd. and then added 16" because there was 16 inches left and that was 412. Then we multiplyed 412 and 381 together and got 156,972. then we multiplyed 156,972 by 31 because we got 31 in a sq. inch and got 4,866,132 blades of grass in the section my teacher marked off.

36 inches
× 11 yds
36
+360
396 inches

396 inches
+ 16 inches
412 inches

412 inches
× 381 inches
412
32960
+123600
156,972 inches

156,972 inches
× 31 blades of grass
156972
4709160
4866,132 blades of grass

1. Answer: 4,866,132 blades of grass.

**Student A's work scored on the *TIMS Multidimensional Rubric:***

| Solving | Level 4 | Level 3 | Level 2 | Level 1 |
|---|---|---|---|---|
| Identifies the elements of the problem and their relationships to one another | All major elements identified | Most elements identified | Some, but shows little understanding of relationships | Few or none |
| Uses problem-solving strategies which are... | Systematic, complete, efficient, and possibly elegant | Systematic and nearly complete, but not efficient | Incomplete or unsystematic | Not evident or inappropriate |
| Organizes relevant information... | Systematically and efficiently | Systematically, with minor errors | Unsystematically | Not at all |
| Relates the problem and solution to previously encountered mathematics and makes connections that are... | At length, elegant, and meaningful | Evident | Brief or logically unsound | Not evident |
| Persists in the problem-solving process... | At length | Until a solution is reached | Briefly | Not at all |
| Looks back to examine the reasonableness of the solution and draws conclusions that are... | Insightful and comprehensive | Correct | Incorrect or logically unsound | Not present |

| Knowing | Level 4 | Level 3 | Level 2 | Level 1 |
|---|---|---|---|---|
| Understands the task's mathematical concepts, their properties and applications... | Completely | Nearly completely | Partially | Not at all |
| Translates between words, pictures, symbols, tables, graphs, and real situations... | Readily and without errors | With minor errors | With major errors | Not at all |
| Uses tools (measuring devices, graphs, tables, calculators, etc.) and procedures... | Correctly and efficiently | Correctly or with minor errors | Incorrectly | Not at all |
| Uses knowledge of the facts of mathematics (geometry definitions, math facts, etc.)... | Correctly | With minor errors | With major errors | Not at all |

| Telling | Level 4 | Level 3 | Level 2 | Level 1 |
|---|---|---|---|---|
| Includes response with an explanation and/or description which is... | Complete and clear | Fairly complete and clear | Perhaps ambiguous or unclear | Totally unclear or irrelevant |
| Presents supporting arguments which are... | Strong and sound | Logically sound, but may contain minor gaps | Incomplete or logically unsound | Not present |
| Uses pictures, symbols, tables, and graphs which are... | Correct and clearly relevant | Present with minor errors or somewhat irrelevant | Present with errors and/or irrelevant | Not present or completely inappropriate |
| Uses terminology... | Clearly and precisely | With minor errors | With major errors | Not at all |

**Figure 16:** *Student A's work and scores on the rubrics*

### Solving

Student A scored a 2 on the Solving dimension. She only partially understood the sampling procedure since she only took one sample. Therefore she did not relate the problem to earlier labs in which students made multiple trials. Furthermore, she did not understand that all she needed was an estimate; an exact answer is not possible. She organized her calculations and showed us her solution. However, she did not give any evidence that she tried to solve the problem in more than one way or look back at her answer to see if it was reasonable.

### Knowing

Student A received a 3 on this dimension. She only partially understood the task, since she did not make multiple trials in her sampling procedure nor use more efficient estimation techniques appropriate to this problem. She translated the problems correctly into symbols, although she did not label her numbers correctly since she did not discriminate between inches and square inches. Her measurements are correct.

### Telling

Since Student A's writing was fairly complete and clear, she scored a 3 on the Telling dimension. She used symbols to show her work correctly although she did not label them with the correct units. She did not use the correct terminology for inches and square inches nor draw a diagram of the solution.

#### Content Note

**Choosing Appropriate Estimation Methods.** Since the calculations in this lesson are estimates, it is appropriate to round numbers to ease computation. For example, Student A could have rounded the number of blades of grass in the sample to 30 blades of grass per square inch and rounded the number of square inches in the grassy area to 150,000 sq in. To find the estimate, she could have simply multiplied 30 × 150,000 to get an estimate of 4,500,000 blades of grass.

**Student B's work:**

We all make an estimation w/ index cards on how many holes their are in square inches in the screen then we add the esitimates and divide by 5 to get the average. Then we figure out how many square inches are in the screen. We multiply the average times how many square inches in the screen and get our answer.

Estimates
18 - 324
17 - 289
16 - 256
14 - 196
15 - 225

÷ 1290
5

Average = 258 sq. in
× 860

221,880

43 inches × 20 inches = 860

The holes in a Screen

1. We cut a square inch out of an index card.

2. Then we put it on the screen and counted the holes in one row. then multiplyed the number twice.

3. We added our estimations together and divided the number by 5 because there are 5 estimations. That is our average 258

4. we measured two of the sides on the screen and multiplyd them together to find out how many square inches there are in the screen

5. Then we multipiyed the square inches by the average we got the answer.

6. the answer is 221,880

That is our estimation we got for how many holes there are in the screen.

**Student B's work scored on the *TIMS Multidimensional Rubric:***

| Solving | Level 4 | Level 3 (circled) | Level 2 | Level 1 |
|---|---|---|---|---|
| Identifies the elements of the problem and their relationships to one another | All major elements identified | X Most elements identified | Some, but shows little understanding of relationships | Few or none |
| Uses problem-solving strategies which are… | Systematic, complete, efficient, and possibly elegant | X Systematic and nearly complete, but not efficient | Incomplete or unsystematic | Not evident or inappropriate |
| Organizes relevant information… | Systematically and efficiently | X Systematically, with minor errors | Unsystematically | Not at all |
| Relates the problem and solution to previously encountered mathematics and makes connections that are… | At length, elegant, and meaningful | X Evident | Brief or logically unsound | Not evident |
| Persists in the problem-solving process… | At length | X Until a solution is reached | Briefly | Not at all |
| Looks back to examine the reasonableness of the solution and draws conclusions that are… | Insightful and comprehensive | Correct | Incorrect or logically unsound | X Not present |

| Knowing | Level 4 (circled) | Level 3 | Level 2 | Level 1 |
|---|---|---|---|---|
| Understands the task's mathematical concepts, their properties and applications… | Completely | X Nearly completely | Partially | Not at all |
| Translates between words, pictures, symbols, tables, graphs, and real situations… | Readily and without errors | X With minor errors | With major errors | Not at all |
| Uses tools (measuring devices, graphs, tables, calculators, etc.) and procedures… | X Correctly and efficiently | Correctly or with minor errors | Incorrectly | Not at all |
| Uses knowledge of the facts of mathematics (geometry definitions, math facts, etc.)… | X Correctly | With minor errors | With major errors | Not at all |

| Telling | Level 4 | Level 3 (circled) | Level 2 | Level 1 |
|---|---|---|---|---|
| Includes response with an explanation and/or description which is… | Complete and clear | X Fairly complete and clear | Perhaps ambiguous or unclear | Totally unclear or irrelevant |
| Presents supporting arguments which are… | Strong and sound | X Logically sound, but may contain minor gaps | Incomplete or logically unsound | Not present |
| Uses pictures, symbols, tables, and graphs which are… | Correct and clearly relevant | X Present with minor errors or somewhat irrelevant | Present with errors and/or irrelevant | Not present or completely inappropriate |
| Uses terminology… | Clearly and precisely | With minor errors | X With major errors | Not at all |

**Figure 17:** *Student B's work and scores on the rubrics*

### Solving

Student B scored a 3 on the Solving dimension. His group understood the sampling procedure, including taking multiple samples and finding the average. He also clearly understood how to find the area of the screen. However, he did not understand that an exact answer is not possible and convenient numbers would be more efficient. Student B persisted in the problem-solving process only until he reached a solution and did not try to find a second strategy or check his answer to see if it is reasonable.

### Knowing

Student B scored a 4 on this dimension. He understood the sampling task and was able to measure and compute correctly. However, he did not always label the numbers in his explanations correctly, and he did not take advantage of more efficient round numbers.

### Telling

Student B's writing was fairly complete and clear, so he earned a 3. We understand how he arrived at his solution, although his description of counting the holes in the screen is somewhat unclear. He uses the division sign in his explanation of finding an average in a nontraditional way, and he did not always label the numbers in the problem correctly.

## Math Facts

DPP items Q and S provide practice with the division facts for the 5s and 10s. DPP Bit Q provides practice dividing round numbers.

## Homework and Practice

- Assign the Journal Prompt as a homework assignment.
- Assign DPP Task R that involves division, number sense, and an understanding of remainders.

## Assessment

- DPP Challenge T can be used to assess fluency in writing remainders as mixed numbers and decimals as well as interpreting remainders.
- Transfer appropriate documentation from the Unit 9 *Observational Assessment Record* to students' *Individual Assessment Record Sheets.*

### Journal Prompt

Explain how you might use a sampling strategy to estimate the number of people in a large crowd.

Estimated Class Sessions

**2**

# At a Glance

## Math Facts and Daily Practice and Problems

DPP items Q and S practice the facts for the 5s and 10s. Items R and T review division and remainders.

## Part 1. Developing a Plan

1. Read and discuss the *Grass Act* Activity Page in the *Student Guide.*
2. Review the student rubrics you will use to assess student work.
3. Students in small groups develop a plan for estimating the number of blades of grass on a lawn. ***(Question 1)***
4. Each student records the group's plan independently. ***(Question 2)***

## Part 2. Solving the Problem

1. Distribute the *Grass Act Questions* Assessment Page from the *Unit Resource Guide.* Tell students which question they are to answer.
2. Students work in groups to collect data needed to solve the problem.
3. Students work independently to find an estimate for the number of blades of grass (holes or loops) in the area of study.
4. You provide feedback on student work.
5. Students revise their work based on your input.
6. Score students' work using the *TIMS Multidimensional Rubric.* Then compare this work to other problems completed earlier in the year.

## Homework

Assign the Journal Prompt for homework.

## Assessment

1. Use DPP Challenge T as an assessment of concepts learned in this unit.
2. Transfer appropriate documentation from the Unit 9 *Observational Assessment Record* to students' *Individual Assessment Record* Sheets.

***Answer Key is on page 114.***

## Notes:

Name ______________________________ Date ____________

# Grass Act Questions

**Your teacher will tell you which of the following problems to solve. After you solve the problem, explain your solution.**

1. Estimate the number of blades of grass in the lawn.
2. Estimate the number of holes in the nylon netting.
3. Estimate the number of holes in the screen.
4. Estimate the number of loops on the towel.

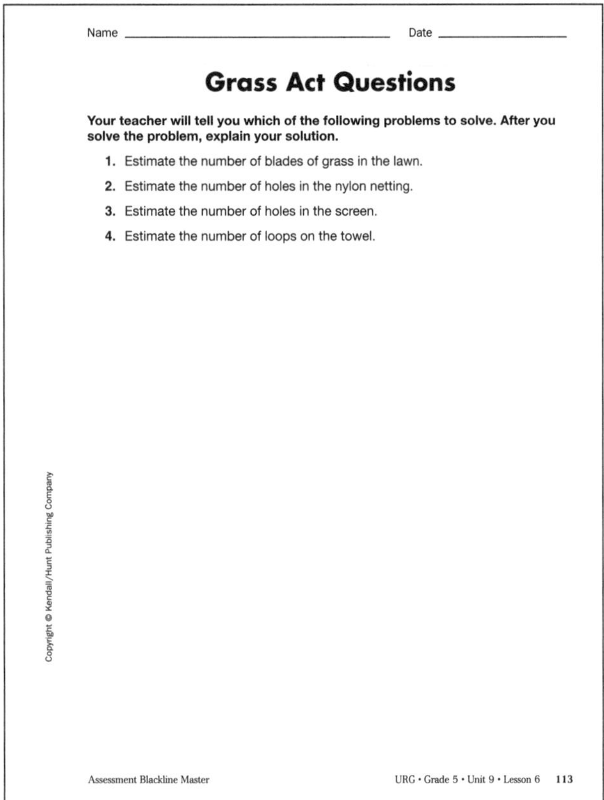

Name ______________________ Date ____________

## Grass Act Questions

**Your teacher will tell you which of the following problems to solve. After you solve the problem, explain your solution.**

1. Estimate the number of blades of grass in the lawn.
2. Estimate the number of holes in the nylon netting.
3. Estimate the number of holes in the screen.
4. Estimate the number of loops on the towel.



Assessment Blackline Master URG • Grade 5 • Unit 9 • Lesson 6 113

***Unit Resource Guide* - page 113**

## Unit Resource Guide (p. 113)

### Grass Act Questions

See Lesson Guide 6 for sample student work and scoring on all three student rubrics.

## Discovery Assignment Book (p. 147)

### Part 1. Division Practice

**A.** 720 R2
Possible strategy: $5762 \div 8 \approx 5600 \div 8$ or 700

**B.** 140 R3

**C.** 1563 R2

**D.** 1063

### Part 2. Fractions and Decimals

**1. A.** $\frac{7}{15} = \frac{21}{45}$ **B.** $\frac{3}{5} = \frac{27}{45}$

**C.** $\frac{1}{3} = \frac{11}{33}$ **D.** $\frac{6}{16} = \frac{66}{176}$

**2. A.** 0.8, 80% **B.** 0.58, 58%

**C.** 0.27, 27%

Name ______ Date ______

**Unit 9** Home Practice

**PART 1 Division Practice**

**Solve each problem using paper and pencil. Estimate to see if your answers are reasonable. Explain your estimation strategy for Question A.**

A. $5762 \div 8 =$ B. $1263 \div 9 =$

C. $4691 \div 3 =$ D. $3189 \div 3 =$

**PART 2 Fractions and Decimals**

1. Find a pair of equivalent fractions in each set. You may use a calculator or another strategy. Be prepared to explain your thinking.

A. $\frac{7}{15}$ $\frac{28}{75}$ $\frac{79}{160}$ $\frac{21}{45}$

B. $\frac{15}{20}$ $\frac{125}{200}$ $\frac{3}{5}$ $\frac{27}{45}$

C. $\frac{1}{3}$ $\frac{33}{100}$ $\frac{4}{5}$ $\frac{11}{33}$

D. $\frac{6}{16}$ $\frac{24}{36}$ $\frac{36}{112}$ $\frac{66}{176}$

2. Use your calculator to change each fraction to a decimal (to the nearest hundredth). Then change each decimal to a percent.

| | Decimal | Percent |
|---|---|---|
| A. $\frac{4}{5}$ | ______ | ______ |
| B. $\frac{7}{12}$ | ______ | ______ |
| C. $\frac{4}{15}$ | ______ | ______ |



CONNECTIONS TO DIVISION DAB • Grade 5 • Unit 9 **147**

*Discovery Assignment Book* - page 147

## Discovery Assignment Book (p. 148)

### Part 3. Multiplication and Division Practice

**A.** 2835 **B.** 36 R5

**C.** 1015 **D.** 365 R11

**E.** 0.26 **F.** 17

**G.** 22.41 **H.** 300

**I.** 187 R28

Name ______ Date ______

**PART 3 Multiplication and Division Practice**

**Solve the following problems using paper and pencil or mental math. Estimate each answer to be sure it is reasonable.**

A. $63 \times 45 =$ B. $221 \div 6 =$ C. $35 \times 29 =$

D. $8406 \div 23 =$ E. $0.52 \times 0.5 =$ F. $918 \div 54 =$

G. $0.83 \times 27 =$ H. $4500 \div 15 =$ I. $12{,}744 \div 68 =$



**148** DAB • Grade 5 • Unit 9 CONNECTIONS TO DIVISION

*Discovery Assignment Book* - page 148

Name ______________________ Date ______________

**PART 4 Using Remainders**

**Solve each of the problems below. Show how you solved each one. Be sure to label the numbers you use, especially your answers.**

Four hundred seventy-eight students from Bessie Coleman School are going to the Lizardland Amusement Park for a day.

1. At the Lizardland Amusement Park the roller coaster has 15 cars. Each car holds 4 people. What is the least number of times it will have to run to give all 478 students a ride?
2. Hot pretzels come in packages of 24. The pretzel stand will prepare two pretzels for each student. The workers at the stand will eat the rest of the pretzels. How many will the workers get to eat?
3. The park workers are putting up banners to welcome the school. They use a whole roll of paper that is 200 feet long for the banners. If they make 16 signs, how long will each sign be?
4. The Lizardland train has cars that can carry 18 passengers. If 250 people are riding the train, how many cars will be full?
5. For each of the problems, write any remainder as a mixed number.

   A. $425 \div 15 =$ B. $3500 \div 50 =$ C. $4005 \div 18 =$





***Discovery Assignment Book* - page 149**

## Discovery Assignment Book (p. 149)

### Part 4. Using Remainders

1. 8 runs
2. 4 pretzels
3. 12.5 feet or $12\frac{1}{2}$ feet
4. 13 cars
5. A. $28\frac{5}{15}$ or $28\frac{1}{3}$
   B. 70
   C. $222\frac{9}{18}$ or $222\frac{1}{2}$

Name ______________________ Date ______________

**PART 5 Solving Problems**

**Choose an appropriate method to solve each of the following problems. For each question, you may choose to use paper and pencil, mental math, or a calculator. Use a separate sheet of paper to explain how you solved each problem. (*Hint:* Drawing a picture may help you solve some of the problems.)**

1. Penny's Pencil Company donated a case of pencils to Bessie Coleman Elementary School. The case contains 48 packs of pencils. Each pack contains 24 pencils. The principal wants to divide the pencils equally among 30 classrooms. How many pencils will each classroom receive? How many pencils will be left over for the office?
2. Mr. Moreno is putting together blank research journals for the fifth grade. Each journal needs 7 sheets of paper. Mr. Moreno has 2 packages of paper to use for the journals. How many journals can he make if one package of paper has 144 sheets?
3. The school is sponsoring a cultural fair. The fifth graders are arranging tables and chairs for a refreshment area at the fair. Half of the tables will seat 8 people. Half of the tables will seat 6 people. They have 112 chairs. How many of each kind of table will they set up?
4. One of the classes is serving burritos at the cultural fair. They will use 3 ounces of cheese on each burrito. How many burritos can they make if they have 5 pounds of cheese? (1 pound = 16 ounces)
5. During the cultural fair a group of students will demonstrate an Irish dance. There are 130 chairs available for the audience. The chairs are arranged into 8 equal rows. How many chairs are in each row? How many extra chairs will there be?
6. A. At the end of the fair, one group of students found that they served 384 egg rolls. The egg rolls came in boxes of 18. How many boxes of egg rolls did they need?
   B. The extra egg rolls were given to the volunteers. How many egg rolls did the volunteers get to share?
   C. If each volunteer got the same number of egg rolls and there were 12 volunteers, how many egg rolls did each volunteer get?
7. A. Mr. Moreno took 78 pictures at the cultural fair. He wanted to arrange the pictures in an album. Each page of his album holds 8 pictures. How many pages of his album can he completely fill?
   B. How many pages will he have to use in all?





***Discovery Assignment Book* - page 150**

## Discovery Assignment Book (p. 150)

### Part 5. Solving Problems

1. There is a total of 1152 pencils. Each classroom will get 38 pencils; 12 pencils will be left over for the office.
2. 41 journals. There will be one sheet of paper left over.
3. 8 of each table.
4. 26 burritos
5. 16 rows 2 chairs left over
6. A. 22 boxes
   B. 6 egg rolls
   C. $\frac{1}{2}$ an egg roll
7. A. 9 pages B. 10 pages

# Glossary

This glossary provides definitions of key vocabulary terms in the Grade 5 lessons. Locations of key vocabulary terms in the curriculum are included with each definition. Components Key: URG = *Unit Resource Guide* and SG = *Student Guide.*

## A

**Acute Angle** (URG Unit 6; SG Unit 6)
An angle that measures less than 90°.

**Acute Triangle** (URG Unit 6 & Unit 15; SG Unit 6 & Unit 15)
A triangle that has only acute angles.

**All-Partials Multiplication Method** (URG Unit 2)
A paper-and-pencil method for solving multiplication problems. Each partial product is recorded on a separate line. (*See also* partial product.)

```
 186
×  3
----
  18
 240
 300
----
 558
```

**Altitude of a Triangle** (URG Unit 15; SG Unit 15)
A line segment from a vertex of a triangle perpendicular to the opposite side or to the line extending the opposite side; also, the length of this line. The altitude is also called the height of the triangle.

**Angle** (URG Unit 6; SG Unit 6)
The amount of turning or the amount of opening between two rays that have the same endpoint.

**Arc** (URG Unit 14; SG Unit 14)
Part of a circle between two points. (*See also* circle.)

**Area** (URG Unit 4 & Unit 15; SG Unit 4 & Unit 15)
A measurement of size. The area of a shape is the amount of space it covers, measured in square units.

**Average** (URG Unit 1 & Unit 4; SG Unit 1 & Unit 4)
A number that can be used to represent a typical value in a set of data. (*See also* mean, median, and mode.)

**Axes** (URG Unit 10; SG Unit 10)
Reference lines on a graph. In the Cartesian coordinate system, the axes are two perpendicular lines that meet at the origin. The singular of axes is axis.

## B

**Base of a Triangle** (URG Unit 15; SG Unit 15)
One of the sides of a triangle; also, the length of the side. A perpendicular line drawn from the vertex opposite the base is called the height or altitude of the triangle.

**Base of an Exponent** (URG Unit 2; SG Unit 2)
When exponents are used, the number being multiplied. In $3^4 = 3 \times 3 \times 3 \times 3 = 81$, the 3 is the base and the 4 is the exponent. The 3 is multiplied by itself 4 times.

**Base-Ten Pieces** (URG Unit 2; SG Unit 2)
A set of manipulatives used to model our number system as shown in the figure below. Note that a skinny is made of 10 bits, a flat is made of 100 bits, and a pack is made of 1000 bits.

**Base-Ten Shorthand** (URG Unit 2)
A graphical representation of the base-ten pieces as shown below.

| Nickname | Picture | Shorthand |
|---|---|---|
| bit | | |
| skinny | | |
| flat | | |
| pack | | |

**Benchmarks** (SG Unit 7)
Numbers convenient for comparing and ordering numbers, e.g., 0, $\frac{1}{2}$, 1 are convenient benchmarks for comparing and ordering fractions.

**Best-Fit Line** (URG Unit 3; SG Unit 3)
The line that comes closest to the points on a point graph.

**Binning Data** (URG Unit 8; SG Unit 8)
Placing data from a data set with a large number of values or large range into intervals in order to more easily see patterns in the data.

**Bit** (URG Unit 2; SG Unit 2)
A cube that measures 1 cm on each edge. 
It is the smallest of the base-ten pieces and is often used to represent 1. (*See also* base-ten pieces.)

## C

**Cartesian Coordinate System** (URG Unit 10; SG Unit 10)
A method of locating points on a flat surface by means of an ordered pair of numbers. This method is named after its originator, René Descartes. (*See also* coordinates.)

**Categorical Variable** (URG Unit 1; SG Unit 1)
Variables with values that are not numbers. (*See also* variable and value.)

**Center of a Circle** (URG Unit 14; SG Unit 14)
The point such that every point on a circle is the same distance from it. (*See also* circle.)

**Centiwheel** (URG Unit 7; SG Unit 7)
A circle divided into 100 equal sections used in exploring fractions, decimals, and percents.

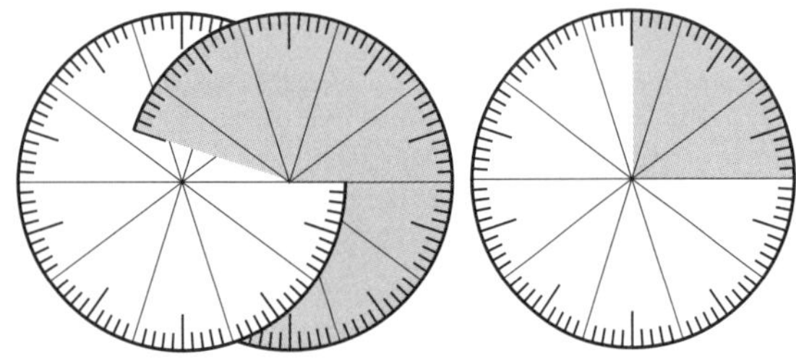

**Central Angle** (URG Unit 14; SG Unit 14)
An angle whose vertex is at the center of a circle.

**Certain Event** (URG Unit 7; SG Unit 7)
An event that has a probability of 1 (100%).

**Chord** (URG Unit 14; SG Unit 14)
A line segment that connects two points on a circle. (*See also* circle.)

**Circle** (URG Unit 14; SG Unit 14)
A curve that is made up of all the points that are the same distance from one point, the center.

**Circumference** (URG Unit 14; SG Unit 14)
The distance around a circle.

**Common Denominator** (URG Unit 5 & Unit 11; SG Unit 5 & Unit 11)
A denominator that is shared by two or more fractions. A common denominator is a common multiple of the denominators of the fractions. 15 is a common denominator of $\frac{2}{3}$ (= $\frac{10}{15}$) and $\frac{4}{5}$ (= $\frac{12}{15}$) since 15 is divisible by both 3 and 5.

**Common Fraction** (URG Unit 7; SG Unit 7)
Any fraction that is written with a numerator and denominator that are whole numbers. For example, $\frac{3}{4}$ and $\frac{9}{4}$ are both common fractions. (*See also* decimal fraction.)

**Commutative Property of Addition** (URG Unit 2)
The order of the addends in an addition problem does not matter, e.g., $7 + 3 = 3 + 7$.

**Commutative Property of Multiplication** (URG Unit 2)
The order of the factors in a multiplication problem does not matter, e.g., $7 \times 3 = 3 \times 7$. (*See also* turn-around facts.)

**Compact Method** (URG Unit 2)
Another name for what is considered the traditional multiplication algorithm.

$$\begin{array}{r} {}^{2\,1}\phantom{0} \\ 186 \\ \times\ 3 \\ \hline 558 \end{array}$$

**Composite Number** (URG Unit 11; SG Unit 11)
A number that has more than two distinct factors. For example, 9 has three factors (1, 3, 9) so it is a composite number.

**Concentric Circles** (URG Unit 14; SG Unit 14)
Circles that have the same center.

**Congruent** (URG Unit 6 & Unit 10; SG Unit 6)
Figures that are the same shape and size. Polygons are congruent when corresponding sides have the same length and corresponding angles have the same measure.

**Conjecture** (URG Unit 11; SG Unit 11)
A statement that has not been proved to be true, nor shown to be false.

**Convenient Number** (URG Unit 2; SG Unit 2)
A number used in computation that is close enough to give a good estimate, but is also easy to compute with mentally, e.g., 25 and 30 are convenient numbers for 27.

**Convex** (URG Unit 6)
A shape is convex if for any two points in the shape, the line segment between the points is also inside the shape.

**Coordinates** (URG Unit 10; SG Unit 10)
An ordered pair of numbers that locates points on a flat surface relative to a pair of coordinate axes. For example, in the ordered pair (4, 5), the first number (coordinate) is the distance from the point to the vertical axis and the second coordinate is the distance from the point to the horizontal axis. (*See also* axes.)

**Corresponding Parts** (URG Unit 10; SG Unit 10)
Matching parts in two or more figures. In the figure below, Sides AB and A′B′ are corresponding parts.

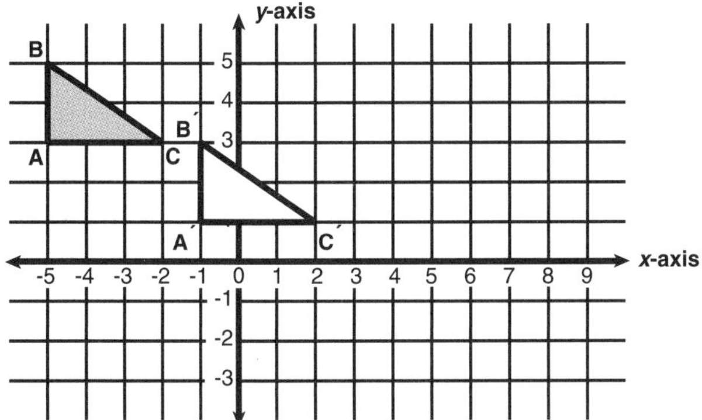


**Cryptography** (SG Unit 11) The study of secret codes.

**Cubic Centimeter** (URG Unit 13)
The volume of a cube that is one centimeter long on each edge.

## D

**Data** (SG Unit 1)
Information collected in an experiment or survey.

**Decagon** (URG Unit 6; SG Unit 6)
A ten-sided, ten-angled polygon.

**Decimal** (URG Unit 7; SG Unit 7)
1. A number written using the base ten place value system.
2. A number containing a decimal point.

**Decimal Fraction** (URG Unit 7; SG Unit 7)
A fraction written as a decimal. For example, 0.75 and 0.4 are decimal fractions and $\frac{75}{100}$ and $\frac{4}{10}$ are the equivalent common fractions.

**Degree** (URG Unit 6; SG Unit 6)
A degree (°) is a unit of measure for angles. There are 360 degrees in a circle.

**Denominator** (URG Unit 3; SG Unit 3)
The number below the line in a fraction. The denominator indicates the number of equal parts in which the unit whole is divided. For example, the 5 is the denominator in the fraction $\frac{2}{5}$. In this case the unit whole is divided into five equal parts. (*See also* numerator.)

**Density** (URG Unit 13; SG Unit 13)
The ratio of an object's mass to its volume.

**Diagonal** (URG Unit 6)
A line segment that connects nonadjacent corners of a polygon.

**Diameter** (URG Unit 14; SG Unit 14)
1. A line segment that connects two points on a circle and passes through the center.
2. The length of this line segment.

**Digit** (SG Unit 2)
Any one of the ten symbols 0, 1, 2, 3, 4, 5, 6, 7, 8, 9. The number 37 is made up of the digits 3 and 7.

**Dividend** (URG Unit 4 & Unit 9; SG Unit 4 & Unit 9)
The number that is divided in a division problem, e.g., 12 is the dividend in $12 \div 3 = 4$.

**Divisor** (URG Unit 2, Unit 4, & Unit 9; SG Unit 2, Unit 4, & Unit 9)
In a division problem, the number by which another number is divided. In the problem $12 \div 4 = 3$, the 4 is the divisor, the 12 is the dividend, and the 3 is the quotient.

**Dodecagon** (URG Unit 6; SG Unit 6)
A twelve-sided, twelve-angled polygon.

## E

**Endpoint** (URG Unit 6; SG Unit 6)
The point at either end of a line segment or the point at the end of a ray.

**Equally Likely** (URG Unit 7; SG Unit 7)
When events have the same probability, they are called equally likely.

**Equidistant** (URG Unit 14)
At the same distance.

**Equilateral Triangle** (URG Unit 6, Unit 14, & Unit 15)
A triangle that has all three sides equal in length. An equilateral triangle also has three equal angles.

**Equivalent Fractions** (URG Unit 3; SG Unit 3)
Fractions that have the same value, e.g., $\frac{2}{4} = \frac{1}{2}$.

**Estimate** (URG Unit 2; SG Unit 2)
1. To find *about* how many (as a verb).
2. A number that is *close to* the desired number (as a noun).

**Expanded Form** (SG Unit 2)
A way to write numbers that shows the place value of each digit, e.g., $4357 = 4000 + 300 + 50 + 7$.

**Exponent** (URG Unit 2 & Unit 11; SG Unit 2 & Unit 11)
The number of times the base is multiplied by itself. In $3^4 = 3 \times 3 \times 3 \times 3 = 81$, the 3 is the base and the 4 is the exponent. The 3 is multiplied by itself 4 times.

**Extrapolation** (URG Unit 13; SG Unit 13)
Using patterns in data to make predictions or to estimate values that lie beyond the range of values in the set of data.

## F

**Fact Families** (URG Unit 2; SG Unit 2)
Related math facts, e.g., $3 \times 4 = 12$, $4 \times 3 = 12$, $12 \div 3 = 4$, $12 \div 4 = 3$.

**Factor Tree** (URG Unit 11; SG Unit 11)
A diagram that shows the prime factorization of a number.

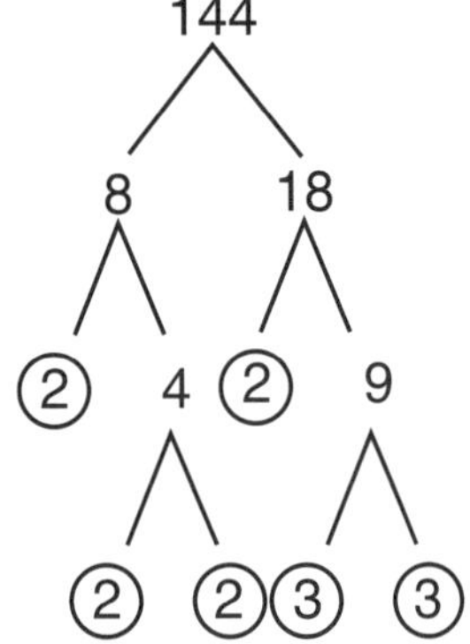


**Factors** (URG Unit 2 & Unit 11; SG Unit 2 & Unit 11)

1. In a multiplication problem, the numbers that are multiplied together. In the problem 3 × 4 = 12, 3 and 4 are the factors.
2. Numbers that divide a number evenly, e.g., 1, 2, 3, 4, 6, and 12 are all the factors of 12.

**Fair Game** (URG Unit 7; SG Unit 7)
A game in which it is equally likely that any player will win.

**Fewest Pieces Rule** (URG Unit 2)
Using the least number of base-ten pieces to represent a number. (*See also* base-ten pieces.)

**Fixed Variables** (URG Unit 4; SG Unit 3 & Unit 4)
Variables in an experiment that are held constant or not changed, in order to find the relationship between the manipulated and responding variables. These variables are often called controlled variables. (*See also* manipulated variable and responding variable.)

**Flat** (URG Unit 2; SG Unit 2)
A block that measures 1 cm × 10 cm × 10 cm. It is one of the base-ten pieces and is often used to represent 100. (*See also* base-ten pieces.)

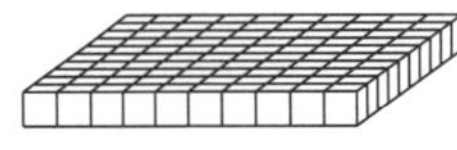

**Flip** (URG Unit 10; SG Unit 10)
A motion of the plane in which the plane is reflected over a line so that any point and its image are the same distance from the line.

**Forgiving Division Method** (URG Unit 4; SG Unit 4)
A paper-and-pencil method for division in which successive partial quotients are chosen and subtracted from the dividend, until the remainder is less than the divisor. The sum of the partial quotients is the quotient. For example, 644 ÷ 7 can be solved as shown at the right.

```
    92
7 ⟌644
   140 | 20
   504
   350 | 50
   154
   140 | 20
    14
    14 |  2
     0   92
```

**Formula** (SG Unit 11 & Unit 14)
A number sentence that gives a general rule. A formula for finding the area of a rectangle is Area = length × width, or $A = l \times w$.

**Fraction** (URG Unit 7; SG Unit 7)
A number that can be written as $a/b$ where $a$ and $b$ are whole numbers and $b$ is not zero.

## G

**Googol** (URG Unit 2)
A number that is written as a 1 with 100 zeroes after it ($10^{100}$).

**Googolplex** (URG Unit 2)
A number that is written as a 1 with a googol of zeroes after it.

## H

**Height of a Triangle** (URG Unit 15; SG Unit 15)
A line segment from a vertex of a triangle perpendicular to the opposite side or to the line extending the opposite side; also, the length of this line. The height is also called the altitude.

**Hexagon** (URG Unit 6; SG Unit 6)
A six-sided polygon.

**Hypotenuse** (URG Unit 15; SG Unit 15)
The longest side of a right triangle.

## I

**Image** (URG Unit 10; SG Unit 10)
The result of a transformation, in particular a slide (translation) or a flip (reflection), in a coordinate plane. The new figure after the slide or flip is the image of the old figure.

**Impossible Event** (URG Unit 7; SG Unit 7)
An event that has a probability of 0 or 0%.

**Improper Fraction** (URG Unit 3; SG Unit 3)
A fraction in which the numerator is greater than or equal to the denominator. An improper fraction is greater than or equal to one.

**Infinite** (URG Unit 2)
Never ending, immeasurably great, unlimited.

**Interpolation** (URG Unit 13; SG Unit 13)
Making predictions or estimating values that lie between data points in a set of data.

**Intersect** (URG Unit 14)
To meet or cross.

**Isosceles Triangle** (URG Unit 6 & Unit 15)
A triangle that has at least two sides of equal length.

## J

## K

## L

**Lattice Multiplication** (URG Unit 9; SG Unit 9)
A method for multiplying that uses a lattice to arrange the partial products so the digits are correctly placed in the correct place value columns. A lattice for 43 × 96 = 4128 is shown at the right.

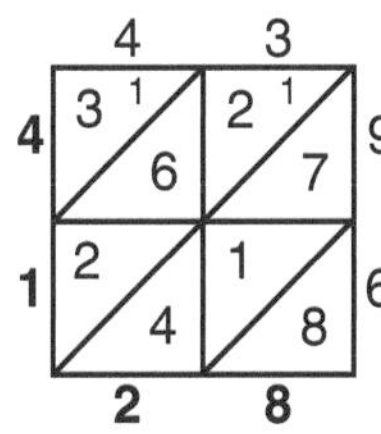

**Legs of a Right Triangle** (URG Unit 15; SG Unit 15)
The two sides of a right triangle that form the right angle.

**Length of a Rectangle** (URG Unit 4 & Unit 15; SG Unit 4 & Unit 15)
The distance along one side of a rectangle.

**Line**
A set of points that form a straight path extending infinitely in two directions.

**Line of Reflection** (URG Unit 10)
A line that acts as a mirror so that after a shape is flipped over the line, corresponding points are at the same distance (equidistant) from the line.

**Line Segment** (URG Unit 14)
A part of a line between and including two points, called the endpoints.

**Liter** (URG Unit 13)
Metric unit used to measure volume. A liter is a little more than a quart.

**Lowest Terms** (SG Unit 11)
A fraction is in lowest terms if the numerator and denominator have no common factor greater than 1.

## M

**Manipulated Variable** (URG Unit 4; SG Unit 4)
In an experiment, the variable with values known at the beginning of the experiment. The experimenter often chooses these values before data is collected. The manipulated variable is often called the independent variable.

**Mass** (URG Unit 13)
The amount of matter in an object.

**Mean** (URG Unit 1 & Unit 4; SG Unit 1 & Unit 4)
An average of a set of numbers that is found by adding the values of the data and dividing by the number of values.

**Measurement Division** (URG Unit 4)
Division as equal grouping. The total number of objects and the number of objects in each group are known. The number of groups is the unknown. For example, tulip bulbs come in packages of 8. If 216 bulbs are sold, how many packages are sold?

**Median** (URG Unit 1; SG Unit 1)
For a set with an odd number of data arranged in order, it is the middle number. For an even number of data arranged in order, it is the mean of the two middle numbers.

**Meniscus** (URG Unit 13)
The curved surface formed when a liquid creeps up the side of a container (for example, a graduated cylinder).

**Milliliter (ml)** (URG Unit 13)
A measure of capacity in the metric system that is the volume of a cube that is one centimeter long on each side.

**Mixed Number** (URG Unit 3; SG Unit 3)
A number that is written as a whole number followed by a fraction. It is equal to the sum of the whole number and the fraction.

**Mode** (URG Unit 1; SG Unit 1)
The most common value in a data set.

**Mr. Origin** (URG Unit 10; SG Unit 10)
A plastic figure used to represent the origin of a coordinate system and to indicate the directions of the $x$- and $y$- axes. (and possibly the $z$-axis).

## N

**N-gon** (URG Unit 6; SG Unit 6)
A polygon with $N$ sides.

**Negative Number** (URG Unit 10; SG Unit 10)
A number less than zero; a number to the left of zero on a horizontal number line.

**Nonagon** (URG Unit 6; SG Unit 6)
A nine-sided polygon.

**Numerator** (URG Unit 3; SG Unit 3)
The number written above the line in a fraction. For example, the 2 is the numerator in the fraction $\frac{2}{5}$. In this case, we are interested in two of the five parts. (*See also* denominator.)

**Numerical Expression** (URG Unit 4; SG Unit 4)
A combination of numbers and operations, e.g., $5 + 8 \div 4$.

**Numerical Variable** (URG Unit 1; SG Unit 1)
Variables with values that are numbers. (*See also* variable and value.)

## O

**Obtuse Angle** (URG Unit 6; SG Unit 6)
An angle that measures more than 90°.

**Obtuse Triangle** (URG Unit 6 & Unit 15; SG Unit 6 & Unit 15)
A triangle that has an obtuse angle.

**Octagon** (URG Unit 6; SG Unit 6)
An eight-sided polygon.

**Ordered Pair** (URG Unit 10; SG Unit 10)
A pair of numbers that gives the coordinates of a point on a grid in relation to the origin. The horizontal coordinate is given first; the vertical coordinate is given second. For example, the ordered pair (5, 3) gives the coordinates of the point that is 5 units to the right of the origin and 3 units up.

**Origin** (URG Unit 10; SG Unit 10)
The point at which the $x$- and $y$-axes intersect on a coordinate plane. The origin is described by the ordered pair (0, 0) and serves as a reference point so that all the points on the plane can be located by ordered pairs.

## P

**Pack** (URG Unit 2; SG Unit 2)
A cube that measures 10 cm on each edge. It is one of the base-ten pieces and is often used to represent 1000. (*See also* base-ten pieces.)

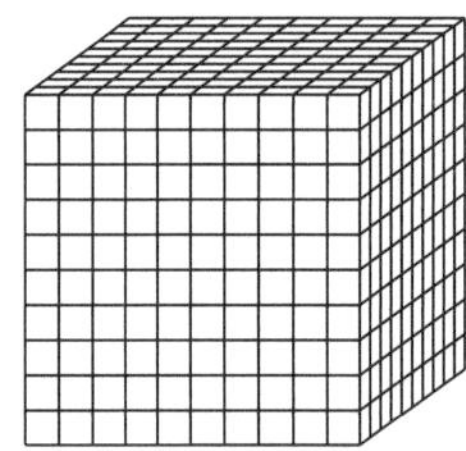

**Parallel Lines** (URG Unit 6 & Unit 10)
Lines that are in the same direction. In the plane, parallel lines are lines that do not intersect.

**Parallelogram** (URG Unit 6)
A quadrilateral with two pairs of parallel sides.

**Partial Product** (URG Unit 2)
One portion of the multiplication process in the all-partials multiplication method, e.g., in the problem 3 × 186 there are three partial products: 3 × 6 = <u>18</u>, 3 × 80 = <u>240</u>, and 3 × 100 = <u>300</u>. (*See also* all-partials multiplication method.)

**Partitive Division** (URG Unit 4)
Division as equal sharing. The total number of objects and the number of groups are known. The number of objects in each group is the unknown. For example, Frank has 144 marbles that he divides equally into 6 groups. How many marbles are in each group?

**Pentagon** (URG Unit 6; SG Unit 6)
A five-sided polygon.

**Percent** (URG Unit 7; SG Unit 7)
Per hundred or out of 100. A special ratio that compares a number to 100. For example, 20% (twenty percent) of the jelly beans are yellow means that out of every 100 jelly beans, 20 are yellow.

**Perimeter** (URG Unit 15; SG Unit 15)
The distance around a two-dimensional shape.

**Period** (SG Unit 2)
A group of three places in a large number, starting on the right, often separated by commas as shown at the right.

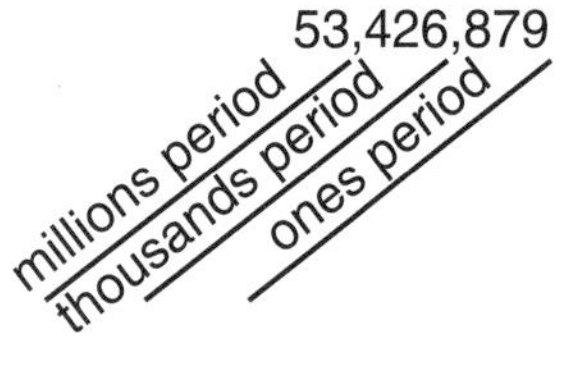


**Perpendicular Lines** (URG Unit 14 & Unit 15; SG Unit 14)
Lines that meet at right angles.

**Pi (π)** (URG Unit 14; SG Unit 14)
The ratio of the circumference to diameter of a circle. π = 3.14159265358979. . . . It is a nonterminating, nonrepeating decimal.

**Place** (SG Unit 2)
The position of a digit in a number.

**Place Value** (URG Unit 2; SG Unit 2)
The value of a digit in a number. For example, the 5 is in the hundreds place in 4573, so it stands for 500.

**Polygon** (URG Unit 6; SG Unit 6)
A two-dimensional connected figure made of line segments in which each endpoint of every side meets with an endpoint of exactly one other side.

**Population** (URG Unit 1 Unit 1)
A collection of persons or things whose properties will be analyzed in a survey or experiment.

**Portfolio** (URG Unit 2; SG Unit 2)
A collection of student work that show how a student's skills, attitudes, and knowledge change over time.

**Positive Number** (URG Unit 10; SG Unit 10)
A number greater than zero; a number to the right of zero on a horizontal number line.

**Power** (URG Unit 2; SG Unit 2)
An exponent. Read $10^4$ as, "ten to the fourth power" or "ten to the fourth." We say 10,000 or $10^4$ is the fourth power of ten.

**Prime Factorization** (URG Unit 11; SG Unit 11)
Writing a number as a product of primes. The prime factorization of 100 is 2 × 2 × 5 × 5.

**Prime Number** (URG Unit 11; SG Unit 11)
A number that has exactly two factors: itself and 1. For example, 7 has exactly two distinct factors, 1 and 7.

**Probability** (URG Unit 7; SG Unit 1 & Unit 7)
A number from 0 to 1 (0% to 100%) that describes how likely an event is to happen. The closer that the probability of an event is to one, the more likely the event will happen.

**Product** (URG Unit 2; SG Unit 2)
The answer to a multiplication problem. In the problem $3 \times 4 = 12$, 12 is the product.

**Proper Fraction** (URG Unit 3; SG Unit 3)
A fraction in which the numerator is less than the denominator. Proper fractions are less than one.

**Proportion** (URG Unit 3 & Unit 13; SG Unit 13)
A statement that two ratios are equal.

**Protractor** (URG Unit 6; SG Unit 6)
A tool for measuring angles.

## Q

**Quadrants** (URG Unit 10; SG Unit 10)
The four sections of a coordinate grid that are separated by the axes.

**Quadrilateral** (URG Unit 6; SG Unit 6)
A polygon with four sides. (*See also* polygon.)

**Quotient** (URG Unit 4 & Unit 9; SG Unit 2, Unit 4, & Unit 9)
The answer to a division problem. In the problem $12 \div 3 = 4$, the 4 is the quotient.

## R

**Radius** (URG Unit 14; SG Unit 14)
1. A line segment connecting the center of a circle to any point on the circle.
2. The length of this line segment.

**Ratio** (URG Unit 3 & Unit 12; SG Unit 3 & Unit 13)
A way to compare two numbers or quantities using division. It is often written as a fraction.

**Ray** (URG Unit 6; SG Unit 6)
A part of a line with one endpoint that extends indefinitely in one direction.

**Rectangle** (URG Unit 6; SG Unit 6)
A quadrilateral with four right angles.

**Reflection** (URG Unit 10)
(*See* flip.)

**Regular Polygon** (URG Unit 6; SG Unit 6; DAB Unit 6)
A polygon with all sides of equal length and all angles equal.

**Remainder** (URG Unit 4 & Unit 9; SG Unit 4 & Unit 9)
Something that remains or is left after a division problem. The portion of the dividend that is not evenly divisible by the divisor, e.g., $16 \div 5 = 3$ with 1 as a remainder.

**Repeating Decimals** (SG Unit 9)
A decimal fraction with one or more digits repeating without end.

**Responding Variable** (URG Unit 4; SG Unit 4)
The variable whose values result from the experiment. Experimenters find the values of the responding variable by doing the experiment. The responding variable is often called the dependent variable.

**Rhombus** (URG Unit 6; SG Unit 6)
A quadrilateral with four equal sides.

**Right Angle** (URG Unit 6; SG Unit 6)
An angle that measures 90°.

**Right Triangle** (URG Unit 6 & Unit 15; SG Unit 6 & Unit 15)
A triangle that contains a right angle.

**Rubric** (URG Unit 1)
A scoring guide that can be used to guide or assess student work.

## S

**Sample** (URG Unit 1)
A part or subset of a population.

**Scalene Triangle** (URG Unit 15)
A triangle that has no sides that are equal in length.

**Scientific Notation** (URG Unit 2; SG Unit 2)
A way of writing numbers, particularly very large or very small numbers. A number in scientific notation has two factors. The first factor is a number greater than or equal to one and less than ten. The second factor is a power of 10 written with an exponent. For example, 93,000,000 written in scientific notation is $9.3 \times 10^7$.

**Septagon** (URG Unit 6; SG Unit 6)
A seven-sided polygon.

**Side-Angle-Side** (URG Unit 6 & Unit 14)
A geometric property stating that two triangles having two corresponding sides with the included angle equal are congruent.

**Side-Side-Side** (URG Unit 6)
A geometric property stating that two triangles having corresponding sides equal are congruent.

**Sides of an Angle** (URG Unit 6; SG Unit 6)
The sides of an angle are two rays with the same endpoint. (*See also* endpoint and ray.)

**Sieve of Eratosthenes** (SG Unit 11)
A method for separating prime numbers from nonprime numbers developed by Eratosthenes, an Egyptian librarian, in about 240 BCE.

**Similar** (URG Unit 6; SG Unit 6)
Similar shapes have the same shape but not necessarily the same size.

**Skinny** (URG Unit 2; SG Unit 2)
A block that measures 1 cm × 1 cm × 10 cm. It is one of the base-ten pieces and is often used to represent 10. (*See also* base-ten pieces.)

**Slide** (URG Unit 10; SG Unit 10)
Moving a geometric figure in the plane by moving every point of the figure the same distance in the same direction. Also called translation.

**Speed** (URG Unit 3 & Unit 5; SG Unit 3 & Unit 5)
The ratio of distance moved to time taken, e.g., 3 miles/1 hour or 3 mph is a speed.

**Square** (URG Unit 6 & Unit 14; SG Unit 6)
A quadrilateral with four equal sides and four right angles.

**Square Centimeter** (URG Unit 4; SG Unit 4)
The area of a square that is 1 cm long on each side.

**Square Number** (URG Unit 11)
A number that is the product of a whole number multiplied by itself. For example, 25 is a square number since 5 × 5 = 25. A square number can be represented by a square array with the same number of rows as columns. A square array for 25 has 5 rows of 5 objects in each row or 25 total objects.

**Standard Form** (SG Unit 2)
The traditional way to write a number, e.g., standard form for three hundred fifty-seven is 357. (*See also* expanded form and word form.)

**Standard Units** (URG Unit 4)
Internationally or nationally agreed-upon units used in measuring variables, e.g., centimeters and inches are standard units used to measure length and square centimeters and square inches are used to measure area.

**Straight Angle** (URG Unit 6; SG Unit 6)
An angle that measures 180°.

## T

**Ten Percent** (URG Unit 4; SG Unit 4)
10 out of every hundred or $\frac{1}{10}$.

**Tessellation** (URG Unit 6 & Unit 10; SG Unit 6)
A pattern made up of one or more repeated shapes that completely covers a surface without any gaps or overlaps.

**Translation**
(*See* slide.)

**Trapezoid** (URG Unit 6)
A quadrilateral with exactly one pair of parallel sides.

**Triangle** (URG Unit 6; SG Unit 6)
A polygon with three sides.

**Triangulating** (URG Unit 6; SG Unit 6)
Partitioning a polygon into two or more nonoverlapping triangles by drawing diagonals that do not intersect.

**Turn-Around Facts** (URG Unit 2)
Multiplication facts that have the same factors but in a different order, e.g., 3 × 4 = 12 and 4 × 3 = 12. (*See also* commutative property of multiplication.)

**Twin Primes** (URG Unit 11; SG Unit 11)
A pair of prime numbers whose difference is 2. For example, 3 and 5 are twin primes.

## U

**Unit Ratio** (URG Unit 13; SG Unit 13)
A ratio with a denominator of one.

**Value** (URG Unit 1; SG Unit 1)
The possible outcomes of a variable. For example, red, green, and blue are possible values for the variable *color.* Two meters and 1.65 meters are possible values for the variable *length.*

**Variable** (URG Unit 1; SG Unit 1)
1. An attribute or quantity that changes or varies. (*See also* categorical variable and numerical variable.)
2. A symbol that can stand for a variable.

**Variables in Proportion** (URG Unit 13; SG Unit 13)
When the ratio of two variables in an experiment is always the same, the variables are in proportion.

**Velocity** (URG Unit 5; SG Unit 5)
Speed in a given direction. Speed is the ratio of the distance traveled to time taken.

**Vertex** (URG Unit 6; SG Unit 6)
A common point of two rays or line segments that form an angle.

**Volume** (URG Unit 13)
The measure of the amount of space occupied by an object.

## W

**Whole Number**
Any of the numbers 0, 1, 2, 3, 4, 5, 6 and so on.

**Width of a Rectangle** (URG Unit 4 & Unit 15; SG Unit 4 & Unit 15)
The distance along one side of a rectangle is the length and the distance along an adjacent side is the width.

**Word Form** (SG Unit 2)
A number expressed in words, e.g., the word form for 123 is "one hundred twenty-three." (*See also* expanded form and standard form.)

## Z